Thomas Sutton

Romance in a Yacht

Thomas Sutton

Romance in a Yacht

ISBN/EAN: 9783744676281

Printed in Europe, USA, Canada, Australia, Japan

Cover: Foto ©Thomas Meinert / pixelio.de

More available books at **www.hansebooks.com**

ROMANCE IN A YACHT

BY

THOMAS SUTTON, B.A.

FORMERLY MEMBER OF THE ROYAL THAMES
AND ROYAL LONDON YACHT CLUBS.

LONDON:

CHAPMAN & HALL, 193, PICCADILLY.

1867.

PREFACE.

THE following Yachting Tale was written within sight and sound of the ocean by one to whom yachting has been a favourite pastime from boyhood. About a dozen years ago he owned a schooner yacht of forty tons, and therefore rather larger than the fictitious BAGATELLE; and he has now a schooner yacht rather smaller. In these two vessels he has visited at different times most of the places alluded to in the tale. He must be permitted to mention these facts, and to ask the reader to accept them as proof of the general truthfulness of the descriptive matter, and of the interest which he himself took in writing this romance.

T. S.

CONTENTS.

ROMANCE IN A YACHT

CHAPTER 1.

ABOUT thirty years ago, in the height of summer, one of those violent circular storms, the nature of which is beginning to be better understood now than it was then, swept over the English Channel, and strewed its shores with wrecks.

This tempest at midsummer lasted three days and four nights. It began with a thunderstorm, and subsided in a flat calm. A sultry and oppressive afternoon was followed by a gorgeous sunset. But the most splendid array of cloud scenery was not in the west, but in the south-east.

A

There Alpine masses of cumulus, deeply dyed with purple and vermillion, were piled up, and illuminated, not from behind but in front by the setting sun. Slowly they spread against the wind over the coppery sky, until they covered it like a pall; and then was seen upon the horizon the first flash of forked lightning, followed at a long interval by a growl of distant thunder. To this first trumpet note of an electric battle between the earth and sky reply was made from the opposite quarter, and soon the lightnings were darting from all sides, and old ocean shook beneath the frequent reverberations of the thunderclaps. To this succeeded a torrent of hail-stones, which seemed to wake the monster —like a parcel of boys pea-shooting a sleeping giant—and he began to ruffle his mane and prepare to take part in the contest. Nor was the true provocative long in coming. First the sigh, and then the whistle, and then the full blast of a hurricane were heard, and the battle of the elements was at its height. During the time the storm lasted, the wind shifted gradually from the south-east, through the southward, and westward, to north-west,—in which quarter it finally fell.

Such was the wild freak of one of those vast eddies in the atmosphere, which are engendered by a sudden rarefaction in the tropics, and which, when they stray into these northern latitudes, do an immensity of mischief in their course.

Now, when a gale of this sort, from the Atlantic, sweeps up the English Channel, there is no spot upon which it wreaks worse violence than the desolate bay of St. Ouen, in the Island of Jersey. This is of some five or six miles in extent, with but little indentation, and it spreads out its arms to the western ocean like a concave mirror to the sun's rays. Here an Atlantic gale meets the first solid obstacle to its mad career, and beaten back into a focus by its own recoil from a high range of sterile sand-hills, which form a background to the bay and a screen to the fertile country beyond, and turned upon itself, it whirls up the loose sand in eddies, and lashes into worse fury a sea which has been already tortured into overfalls by the rushing of a swift tide over a rocky bed. Nor is this all, for even when the winds are hushed, heavy rollers, through which it is impossible to launch a boat, and which have been compared without exaggeration to the surf at Madras, come

tumbling in with every flood tide, and make
a bellowing that may be heard over the whole
island, even to the little town of Gorey, which
is twelve miles distant on its opposite side.
Imagine then the scene which this wild coast
must have presented on the morning of the
departure of the hurricane which has just been
described!

But dreary and barren as is St. Ouen's Bay—
though not without a certain solemn beauty of
its own—it is still thinly inhabited by a hardy
race of fishermen, vraickers, and little farmers,
whose dwellings and appointments are indicative
of their semi-barbarous mode of life. Near its
Northern extremity, and within the partial shelter
of some high cliffs, is a cluster of stiff ugly stone
houses, with red-tiled roofs, forming the village of
L'Etacq; and within a similar nook at its Southern
extremity lie ensconced a few detached cottages,
which constitute the still humbler village of
La Pulente. The former of these is inhabited
chiefly by fishermen, who moor their boats, for
want of a proper harbour, across a sort of natural
roadway that exists within a flat reef of half-
tide rocks, in which exposed spot they lie
broadside to the sea, moored by strong chains

from bow and stern. As for the inhabitants of La Pulente—as nature has been less bountiful to them in the matter of a harbour, however rough—they seem rather to eschew boating, and to prefer earning a hard livelihood in a more regular and less exciting way, by the collection of sea-weed, or vraic, which is highly prized for manure. The two villages are about four miles apart; and between them is the gentle curve of a hard flat sandy beach, fringed at high-water mark with a bank of slate-coloured pebbles. Near the edge of this, on the land side, are dotted at regular intervals a row of martello towers, two of which have been undermined by the sea within the last ten years. Between these now useless military works, and the high ridge of sand-hills before alluded to, is a common, which reminds one, on a small scale, of the Roman Campagna; for when the shadows of the summer clouds flit across it on a sunny day, it requires but little stretch of fancy to imagine those sand-hills the range of Appenines, and the blue waters of the Channel the Mediterranean on the west. Such, at least, is a dream in which the writer of these lines has indulged, whilst wandering in a rather favourite bay. On the common, which may be half a mile wide in its broadest part, may be seen, at all times of the year, lean horses and heifers tethered, cropping the stunted herbage within the circle that their rope allows; while immediately beneath the sand-hills, and in such more fertile spots as are found between their spurs which stretch out upon the plain, are a few homesteads, with an enclosed field or two around, where the owners of the aforesaid animals reside, and make their butter, and rear their pig, and grow cabbages and onions for their conger soup, and barley and rye, potatoes and turnips for their own consumption and that of their live stock.

Such is the present aspect of St. Ouen's Bay; nor is it probable that it has varied greatly from this for centuries past, for it is a spot which civilization is not likely to invade too closely, and where nature seems resolved to have it all her own way. It only remains to add to this description of the Western wilderness of Jersey— an island which is otherwise remarkable for much attractive beauty and luxuriance of scenery — that steep granite cliffs, and formidable reefs stretching far out to sea, guard both its Northern and Southern extremities; while, as if these, and the heavy surf upon the beach were not thought enough of themselves to scare away an invading foe, a strong tower, mounted with guns, has been erected upon a rocky islct called La Rocco, near the centre of the bay, which is accessible on foot only at low water spring tides.

CHAPTER 2.

THE OLD MAN OF LA PULENTE.

IT wanted about an hour to sunrise on the day of the abatement of the gale described in the preceding chapter, and the short darkness of a midsummer night was still brooding over land and sea, when, notwithstanding the early hour, an old man and his daughter, a woman of middle age, were already astir, and looking out anxiously over the troubled ocean from a small attic window in the gable end of one of the cottages at La Pulente. The attention of the old man, ever on the alert during a westerly gale, had been already attracted by an object in the offing, indistinctly seen, and which he believed to be a vessel dismasted and waterlogged; and he had called to his daughter to assist him with her younger eyes in making it out. The two were therefore eagerly engaged in watching, as well as the darkness would permit, the movements of the floating body, whatever it might be, while they speculated on the chances of its being driven ashore beneath their very window, and longed for the advent of daylight to clear up the mystery concerning it.

The cottage in question, which was named La Bie, resembled most of the others in the place, —that is to say, its walls were of rough stone, its roof of red tiles with a high pitch, and its shape a simple box, with a gable at each end, one of which was surmounted by a chimney stack of red brick; but it stood apart from the rest, and nearer to the edge of the beach, so as to command a better sea view. Like many other cottages in Jersey, instead of facing the road by the side of which it stood, it was placed at right angles to it, so that, as the road ran parallel to the shore, one gable end of the cottage, viz., that in which the attic window was, exactly faced the sea. Behind the cottage were the usual lean-to and outhouse; and around it was a sandy garden, a large portion of which was devoted to the cultivation of pinks, wallflowers, and stocks, to the exclusion of the cabbage and potatoe. With the exception, then,

B

of the rather unusual produce of the garden, this tenement resembled externally the other humble dwellings in La Pulente. The same must also be said of the two rooms on the ground floor, one of which was a kitchen. The appointments and general appearance of these rooms were the same as those of the other cottages in the place. There was the same wide and deep hearth for burning furze and sea-weed, with its large swing boiler, its trivet, and its heap of vraic ashes. There were the same dirty floors, and grimy walls and ceiling ; the same old carved corn-chest which collectors of curiosities prize so highly ; the same ricketty chairs, and round tables with two flaps ; and the same gaudy pictures of Napoleon the First, and Mr. T. P. Cook as William, in Black-Eyed Susan, which are to be found in most cottages of this class. But the two lower rooms were considered public ones, in which a neighbour might at any time enter; and the old man alluded to, who had purchased the cottage two years before, had also included in the purchase the furniture of those rooms, and had allowed it to remain as he found it. The attics above, which were approached by a narrow step-ladder, were considered strictly private ; and there, strange to say, the appointments were widely different from those in the rooms below, and such as to let the visitor at once into the secret that the old man and his daughter had belonged to a higher class than the peasantry about them, and were people of some education and taste. The daughter, at any rate, possessed the lady-like virtue of cleanliness, as shown by the general order and neatness of these two attics. That in which her father slept is worthy of particular description.

Its floor was fastidiously clean, and its walls neatly whitewashed, as well as the under side of the tiles, which were simply pointed with mortar and exposed to view. The old man was bedridden, and never left this room, so that he had all those chattels about him which he required. His bed was a large low chest, or ottoman, on castors; and its counterpane was a green and black woollen one, very thick and handsome, and of French manufacture. The furniture seemed to have belonged mostly to a ship's cabin: and on the shelves against the walls were rolls of charts, as well as some law books, the Newgate Calendar, and novels. The window commanded a view over the entire bay, and the bed was placed immediately under it, and so that its occupant could look out of it as he lay. In order to prevent a draught from entering through any joint or cranny, a single large pane of plate glass had been puttied into the window frame itself, solid, so as not to open; and in order that a telescope might be used, a corner of this pane had been cut off, and the space covered by a wooden panel, in which there was a round hole to admit of the glass being passed through. It will readily be believed that the chief delight of the bedridden old man, when not otherwise employed over his books and papers, consisted in looking out upon the ocean from this little window, and watching the vessels as they passed.

The cottagers of La Pulento were but little aware of the kind of neighbour they had amongst them, for as he was never seen about, his existence and habits could only be known to them through such information as his daughter chose to impart; and that was the least possible, as she had no inducement to be communicative on that topic. The various articles of furniture which the attics contained had been originally introduced into the house wrapped up in old sails and matting, and no surmises had been excited on that score. As for the lady herself, she had soon adopted in her dress the picturesque and convenient fashions of the place, and she performed without help the menial offices of their little ménage, without apparent reluctance or affectation. Nevertheless, there is gossiping even in such places as La Pulente; and wiseacres, who take a delight in illnatured scandal, would sometimes whisper stories to the discredit of the Smiths, of La Bie. There was a report afloat that the old man and his daughter were not so much the victims of a seeming poverty, as exiles from society for a far less worthy cause; and it was even hinted that old Smith's seclusion from the world did not proceed so much from his being bed-ridden, which was a sham, as from his wish to escape a hempen collar round his neck; and that the truth would leak out some day. These insinuations were, however, received by the more sensible and good-natured of the neighbours as a joke; for the daughter Hannah, at any rate, was a good kind soul, against whom no cause of ill-feeling existed; whilst all that could be positively known about the old man was that he often received letters and parcels by the post, and occasionally a visit from a fisherman whose occupation lay on the opposite side of the island. To which may be added, that the Smiths, however reduced their circumstances might be, always paid their humble way with scrupulous punctuality.

Daylight came at last; and while the old man and his daughter were still watching from their attic window the fate of what then proved really to be a small vessel in distress, their neighbours were hurrying down to the shore to be present at the crisis of the wreck; for she was evidently drifting fast into the bay, and seemed nearly certain to go to pieces in the surf, or on the rocks.

CHAPTER 3.

—

THE BAGATELLE IN THE SURF.

OLD Smith was directing his telescope towards the group of people on the beach, as well as towards the various footpaths and cart-tracks which led down to it, rather than to the vessel which was the object of general attention.

"I don't see Jim and Joe about anywhere," he remarked, with the glass still at his eye, and addressing his daughter.

"But I do," she replied. "They have just this instant gone down the slip, to join the other people."

"Ha, so they have," said her father, looking in the direction indicated. "I knew they'd be coming down here, pretty smart, as soon as the gale took off. Where the carcase is there will the eagles be gathered together. But why did they pass our cottage without coming up to see me? Run and stop them, Hannah, and say I want to speak to them directly."

As he gave this order, somewhat harshly, he took his eye from the telescope and glanced at his daughter's face. It was a good kind honest one, and pleasant to look at; but its expression at that moment was one of painful anxiety for the fate of the ship, mingled with some other momentary feeling which her father's remarks had aroused. This he perceived as their eyes met, and instantly added, in a gentler tone

" We may have a chance, Hannah, of doing a good and a Christian deed this day. That unfortunate ship is doomed, and will strike the ground in a few minutes; then the first sea that breaks over her will sweep those two poor creatures off the deck—you see them, don't you?—and their bodies, dead or alive, will be flung ashore by the rising tide. Now, when the crisis comes in the fate of those poor things, I foresee that nothing whatever will be done, by that gaping crowd of lookers-on, to save them. There will be plenty of shouting, no doubt, and hurry-scurry, and rushing this way and that, and tumbling over each other, and getting wet up to their knees, and wringing of hands, and sympathy loudly expressed,—but nothing will be done that is of any use, except to the dead bodies, when it is too late to save life. But perhaps the old cripple lying here may help the poor things with a little forethought and common sense. So run, my girl, and send up Jim and Joe at once to me, and then light a fire, and put on lots of furze, and all the pans you can get full of water, and make it boil quick—for hot water will be wanted, Hannah, as soon as you can get it—mark my words!"

With this exhortation the good woman went off on her errand of benevolence, with the speed of one who is in earnest in a good work; and in a couple of minutes the aforesaid Jim and Joe stood before the doorway of La Bie.

These two—the former a man, the latter a lad, were the only human beings in Jersey who were known to be admitted to any sort of intimacy with the Smiths; and even they were not frequent visitors to La Pulenté. Jim was a thick-set strong-built sailor, about forty years of age, who gained his living during the Winter on board an oyster dredger at Gorey, and during the Summer months by mackerel and conger fishing, and trawling, in the same craft. The boy Joe was the kind of young chap you may see in any coasting or fishing smack that hails from an English port. But why these two sailor-fellows should be connected in any way with the Smiths, no one could exactly divine. Of course, Jim had been questioned on the subject by his pals, both directly and indirectly, but without getting anything out of him that was really to the point. And yet he was by no means a reserved or taciturn man. On the contrary, he was considered a sociable and highly communicative chap; and the offer of a glass of grog, or a handful of baccy would at any time provoke him into spinning a long yarn. "Come now, old shipmate," a comrade would say, as they sat together over the fire in their little caboose, "tell us true, on your honour like a man, who is that rum old fogey that you go to see so slyly up at La Pulente?" "Well then," Jim would answer, "I'll tell you—I will, so help me Bob. But pour a fellow out another glass first, and let me fill a fresh pipe." Then would follow a marvellous tale, the only fault of which would be that it bore no sort of resemblance in any particular to a dozen others, on the same topic, that the same narrator had told before, with an equally solemn asseveration of their truth. The fact is, Jim had a talent for romance, and to such an extent that he had gained for himself, by the liberal exercise of it, the nickname of "lying Jim;" but that was always *sotto voce*, for he was a strong chap, and choleric withal, and sometimes affected much sensitiveness on points of honour. "Jim of the Peggy," or "Jim of the Jersey Maid," or "Jim of the Jupiter," was his more common name, according to the smack he might belong to at the time; for his surname no one had ever heard, or what his antecedents were either. He was a strong, ruddy, weather-beaten-visaged Englishman, with sandy hair and whiskers, and a blue eye that had a wicked twinkle in it at times, but with which he could look you honestly in the face, nevertheless. On the present occasion, he had been up all night, and was invested in his roughest seaman's garb, viz., a red night-cap, three blue woollen Guernseys, one over the other, two pair of trousers, and strong top-boots well greased. Such was the man Jim in dress, features, form, and idiosyncrasy. As for Joe, he was no relation of the other's, and a lazy lad, who knew nothing but just how to pull and haul as he was told, but with plenty of cheek nevertheless.　He was Jim's satellite, and that is all that need be said.

The two quickly mounted the step ladder to Old Smith's room, and presented themselves before him.　He was at the time looking intently through his glass at the drifting vessel, which was then getting pretty close in shore.　He merely said to the lad, as they entered, "Go down, Joe, and help my daughter," and bestowed not a syllable of greeting upon Jim.　But the latter was not in the least abashed at this cool reception, but took it all in good part.　He walked up to the old man's bedside, and accosted him boldly with the following rigmarole—every word of which happened to be true:

"Good morning, your honour.　I was coming up here—I was, so help me Bob,—but I just wanted to have a close view of the little vessel first, and hear if any o' them chaps knew anything about her.　I've been watching her for the last half-hour, as I came down the côtil.　My eyes, didn't it blow last night !　But Lor', we didn't feel it where I was, as you do here.　Why I was aboard all night, at anchor off Gorey,

playing cards with another chap, and there was
no sea on a bit,—but here—my eyes, isn't that
a surf! How she will hammer at it when
her keel takes the ground—and what'll become
of them two poor creturs aboard? That's what
I want to know—ain't they in a precious mess?
She's a yacht—and one of them long legged
ones, I'll be bound, that draws as much water
as a 500-ton ship deep loaded—and that man
and woman aboard of her looks to me like a
gen'l'man and his wife—perhaps the owner—
and there's a young babby too. You've seen
'em all, your honor, ain't you? But what's
become of the crew?—that's what I can't
make out. I reckon they deserted her in the
gig, for I can't see any boats aboard—but they
made a nasty job of it, I know. Well, if I
was aboard of her now, I'd just peel off and
take to my fins, that's what I'd do—a fellow'd
have just half a chance of his life that way—
but then there's the woman to look after—he
couldn't leave her behind. Bother me now, but
if I had our dingey here, I'd try and get off
to 'em somehow—but the chaps hereabouts are
afeard to launch a boat. Do you see, your honour,
how the gale's gone down all at once? I never

see'd such a thing in all my life—and I've seen many gales of wind too—but there's a mortal sea on yet—it'll go down with the ebb tide though—it soon goes down on soundings—it ain't like the main ocean here, is it your honour, you know that? Can you make any more out, your honour? That man on board the wreck has been up and down twenty times—but I've only seen the woman put her head up once, with the babby in her arms, poor thing! He chucked out an anchor—he's a terrible strong young chap—but Lor' the cable parted with the first pitch she gave—I'll get that anchor at low water—you see if I don't—that'll be worth three pound. Then he set a sort of staysail on her, between the stump of the foremast, and the main cross-trees, with the main haulyard blocks—but Lor' the sail wouldn't draw a bit—there ain't a breath of wind now, and the tide was heaving her right in. She's done for—that's sure enough. But I say, your honour, you ain't offended with me, are you? I was coming up to see you—in course I was."

" Offended, Jim? Stuff," replied the old man. " Do you take me for Beau Brummel, or Talleyrand, that I'm always bound to be polite?

I sent for you, man, to try and see what we could do to help those two poor creatures and the child. She'll strike soon. She looks to me not more than forty tons, but I dare say she draws eleven feet of water aft. The heel of her stern post will strike first—then she'll slew round broadside to it—and the first sea that strikes her, down she'll go upon her bilge—she'll never rise again —and then the seas will make a clean breach over all. But we must try and save those people, Jim."

And as he said it, he grasped the sailor's thick forearm with his bony fingers, and looked earnestly in his face, adding,

" You've got the muscle, Jim, and I've got the brains—that's a law of nature—she couldn't give either of us the muscles and the brains both—that would be too much—a man who had them both would be too dangerous, and his fellows would join to strangle him when they found him out—but she has given *you* the muscles, Jim, and *me* the brains—you are the machine, and I'm the engineer—so now attend. Don't try to think for yourself, but do just as I tell you. It will be for your own good, I promise you, you pig, as well as theirs ; and a good deed done this day will weigh in the balance of the King of Kings, when your soul and mine, Jim, stand shivering before the Judgment Seat. Now don't grin at me, you idiot—for what I say is true, and you know it is."

But Jim did grin a great deal; and wasn't offended in the least at being called an idiot, and a pig, and a machine. He replied good-naturedly

"You talk just like a parson, your honour; and I always said they ought to have sent you to a college for them sort of covies, instead of where they did. But that's neither here nor there. I've got muscles, sure enough—and if I could but get a fair grip of them poor creturs, if it was only with my eyelids, I'd soon have 'em all ashore, safe enough. Trust me for pulling and hauling, if that'd save 'em—but how to hook on to 'em—that's the rub."

"Help me off this bed," said the old man, "and I'll soon show you how."

"Well, that *is* a good 'un," said Jim, ironically.

"You scoundrel," answered the other angrily. "Hav'n't I told you a hundred times that about ten years ago I broke both legs, compound fractures. It is true the bones may have joined again, but the marrow has always been diseased, and it always aches, except when I have no sensation in it at all. Do you think I should be the cowardly poltroon to lie here all my life, if I could walk about?"

"I beg your honour's pardon," said Jim, helping him off his couch, "but I *have* seen you hop about once, smart enough."

"Lift up that lid," said the old man sharply, pointing to the top of the ottoman which formed his bed, "and take out the bow and arrow, and the coil of line that you will find inside."

Jim did as he was told; and said a word or two which proved his comprehension of the scheme. Then, with the above implements in his hands, he took himself off, and was soon seen hurrying across the sands to where the crowd had collected to watch the fate of the unfortunate yacht, and of the helpless beings upon her deck.

It was full ten minutes before the vessel grounded; and during that time Hannah and Joe had lighted a roaring furze fire, and put on pans of water to boil. The former then rejoined her father at the window, who was eagerly watching the fate of the yacht.

"She has touched the ground at last," he said, excitedly. "Look, girl, look with all your eyes. Bravo, Jim—well shot—the man on board has caught the line—see—the woman has got a life-belt on—a capital idea that—and he is tying the end of the line to it, so as not to chafe her flesh—Bravo—that's right—and see— she's holding the baby tight between her arms— none but a mother would do that now. But here comes a heavy surge—off with you all, poor things—haul away, Jim—in with them—haul, I say, with all your might and main."

"Oh God, have mercy on them," cried Hannah, with her two hands pressed together in the attitude of prayer.

"That was a smasher," continued the old man, —"what a sea it is—right over all—where are they now? I can't see one of 'em. Yes I can— there's the baby gone adrift—why, you mother, couldn't you keep firmer hold of your little one than that?—it's parted from you now for ever— you'll never clasp it in your arms again—alive at at least—never, never! But the man—what's become of him? Oh, I see him—there he is— striking out—good heavens, and in such a surf— close to the child, too—but that's no good—look to yourself, my poor fellow—never mind the child now—it 'll take all your strength and pluck to save yourself—the child 's as good as lost. No, it isn't—it floats bravely, like a cork—the roll of flannel round it keeps it up—and I see the man pushing it before him—bravo—fine fellow—why they 're as good as half way in already. But stand by—here comes another smasher—what a monster—right over all again—where are they all now?—the woman I can't see a bit—but Jim keeps hauling something in—go easy, man— you 'll smother her—give her time to breathe— don't keep her under too long—twenty seconds are enough to drown. Now I see the child again —bravo—and there 's the man close to it, pushing it along again—what a time a roll of flannel will keep up—brave fellow, that man, Hannah—see how he 's striking out—how he sticks to it, to save the child—why he 's almost now within his depth—you lubbers standing there, why don't you rush in and bear a hand— fling a rope, or anything. Well done, lads— didn't I say so—in they go, sure enough—one, two, three of them, hand in hand. But look out—here comes another smasher—over all again —they retreat, the caitiffs—oh fie, you dogs. I say, Hannah, respectable men those, very ; how they do take care of number one. I wish poor Coles was here, the thief, who got seven years, poor vagabond—he 'd soon have 'em out— a thief, but with grand instincts, poor devil. Your thieves and vagabonds for me, and none of your too respectable men, I say—sharks, and pigs, and monkeys, all of 'em—I hate the lot sometimes. But see—by heavens he touches bottom now— and in they all go again, up to their necks, this time—well done lads—now they 've got hold of him, child and all—and Jim has hauled out the woman too—he 's got her in his arms—capital, that 's first-rate. Now Hannah, girl, it 's your turn next—didn't I tell you so ?—see to the hot water, quick—the woman looks exhausted— dead, I think—and bleeding from the head. Here they come with her—make haste, Hannah girl—be quick, quick, quick."

The above disjointed sentences describe exactly what occurred.

For a few instants after the woman was hauled ashore, the entire crowd collected round her; and then it separated into two groups, forming two processions which moved quickly towards the slip. First, came the man who had saved himself and the child, bearing it in his arms, and hurrying on before the rest, followed by half-a-dozen of the lookers-on, mostly women; and then followed Jim, and the remainder, carrying the body of the woman, with extreme care. Hannah went to meet the first group, and led them into the kitchen of the cottage; and the rest soon followed, and went with the body into the other ground floor room.

The old man in the attic could see no more, but as the door was open he heard much of what was going on below. At first there was a buzz of voices, and much hurrying to and fro,—in the midst of which an infant's cries were heard. Then the voices became more subdued, and almost sank into a whisper, while the footsteps became less frequent, and more solemn in their tread; until at length, most of the good people had left the house, and formed themselves into little groups outside, discussing with solemn faces something tragic that oppressed their hearts. The child was living; but the woman, what was she? The old man's sense of hearing was acute, and he listened most intently, but no one ever thought of *him*. Still, he knew the full meaning of every sound he heard, and guessed too truly what was going on in the room beneath that in which he lay—the creak of tables drawn into the middle of it—the lifting of a body upon them—the hanging of a sail before the window—and the mutterings of women who were laying out a corpse. He knew what such sounds boded, and needed none to tell him that the child was living, but that its mother was no more!

A full hour then elapsed, and at last Jim went up to the old man—him with brains and forethought, whom the machines without either had never once thought it worth their while to go to, and consult.

The rough sailor seated himself upon the bed, and there was deep grief, and something very like a tear in his blue eye. But the old man looked cold and stern. His excitement was over —he had been mortified by their neglect—and there was no longer any show of feeling in his face. He had come to think only of himself.

"It's all up, your honour, with that poor thing," said Jim, at last, in broken accents, very different from his common blunt defiant tone. "I know'd, as soon as I touched her that she was stone dead. She wasn't drowned, but killed by something which smashed in her poor head—

poor little darling—pretty cretur—wasn't she a beauty—and to die like that—so young!"

Here the good fellow brushed off a tear with his sleeve, and then continued his lament.

" And so straight and slim—with long black curly hair, and little soft white hands—such a pictur'—and there she lies now—cold and dead—on the tables just below us. We 've laid her out, all ready for the inquest—and the parson 's been here—and the doctor too—but Lor', what good can they do now ?"

" How about the child, and the young man ? Are *they* all right ?" asked Smith.

But Jim didn't heed the question. He went on.

" It was all my fault, I 'm half afeard— pulling and hauling too hard at first. Bother that nasty bow of your's—if I hadn't sent 'em a line, it wouldn't have happened. She had a life-belt on—and she 'd soon have come ashore— the tide would have washed her up safe enough— just like the rest. Any fool might have known that—but I 've smashed the nasty thing—bother your engineering, old man, I say—let natur' do her work. Poor thing—I sha' n't never get her out of my thoughts—she 'll lie on my heart like a pig of cold iron ballast,—and I 've got enough of that sort aboard already, God knows."

"For the *second* time of asking, how about the father, and the child?" demanded the old man, angrily, adding, "Let the dead bury their dead—what is that to us?"

"Lor', your honour—they 're all right—didn't you hear 'em? they made noise enough—I never see 'd a man take on as that young chap did at first—but he soon came cool enough, and then all his thoughts were about the child. She 's quite safe—it 's a little girl—we 've got a young woman come to nurse it—and she 's to stay here with your daughter for ever so long—it 's all arranged—and they 're to have the room below."

"The devil they are," retorted Smith.

"Well—and why not, I should like to know, old growler," replied Jim. "If your daughter chooses to turn an honest penny by looking after that child—what 's that to you. Better that a hundred times than....."

"You simpleton, you pig, you everlasting idiot," retorted the old man. "Ask yourself rather, what is that to you? Is anything of to-day's work anything to you? If it is, give up blubbering, and look to yourself. Tell me. now, what have you learnt about the man, the child, the yacht? By twelve o'clock she'll be high and dry. What then, eh? I think I know. Shall I tell you what will happen? Why just this. Let us go through it all from the very first. When she grounded, and slewed round broadside on, that sea that swept them off went clean over her and filled her, and down she went. There she lies now, safe enough, and you can just see her mast head. Her V-bottom saved her from hammering herself to pieces in the surf. If she'd had a flat floor, she would have been knocked about, and hove right up to high water mark, and stove in, and shattered to matches and shivereens. But now, when the tide goes down you'll find her not hurt a bit. But what will happen next? Why a lot of fellows will get round her, and tip each other the wink, and tear her copper off, and prig, and do nothing to save her from becoming a total wreck—for the sooner she breaks up the better luck for them. But that won't do for *us*—for you and *me*, I mean—mark *that*."

"It ain't unlikely," answered Jim, "but there's time enough to think of that. *I*'m most in with the gen'l'man, and *I* mean to have the first chance. He's gone down on the sands just now, to look at her, and if I don't go after him, and pitch something into him that'll make him wide awake, my name's not——."

" Go and pitch yourself to——, ungrateful hound," cried the old man, passionately. "What's that to *me?*"

"I say, old growler, none of that," replied the sailor, with an angry spot upon his cheek. "I won't stand too much of that—I won't, by——. You got out o' bed the wrong way this morning. Take care—or I'll make you get out a worse way yet."

So saying, he flung himself out of the room—slammed the door—went heavily down the step-ladder, and left the house.

" Hannah," called out the old man, as soon as Jim was gone. " Come here, I want you."

She came at once.

" What have you been about all this time?" he demanded, pettishly.

" My poor father," she replied, " I'm so sorry I couldn't come to you before—but we've all been in a peck of trouble down below."

" Stuff—I know it.   Go and fetch the gentleman up here at once.   I want to see him, and I
must see him, and I *ought* to have seen him long
ago.   You'll let that scoundrel Jim have the
first chance."

" I was afraid, my father, to show him up,
until I had had a word with you about it first."

" Pooh, girl! What, do you think I care for
that ?   Show him up here at once."

She carried the message quickly, and the
gentleman left the side of Jim, who had already
joined him, and returned with her to the cottage.

CHAPTER 4.

**FIRST SUSPICIONS.   THE BAGATELLE LEFT HIGH
AND DRY.**

THE stranger mounted the step ladder to the
attic in which the old man lay, and presented
himself at the open door, but paused a minute
before he entered, in a state of much surprise at
seeing an apartment within the roof, so superior
in its appointments to those below.   On the
other hand, the curious spectacle which he
himself presented was as closely scrutinized by
the old man.   On leaving the vessel for his
struggle in the surf, he had simply worn a pair
of swimming drawers and canvas shoes, in
order not to throw away a chance for life.   The
shoes he still had on, but the drawers had been
exchanged for a pair of Jim's overalls; in
addition to which he had also borrowed a
Guernsey from the latter, and a rough pilot

coat from another sailor. Nevertheless, in this rude garb, and with his hair matted with salt water, he still looked, what in truth he was, and what no attire could ever have concealed, a gentleman, and a handsome young fellow also, tall and strongly built. On the other hand, the old man was sufficiently picturesque too, and not more carefully got up as regarded toilet, than his visitor. Over his shoulders was cast a thick scarlet knitted woollen cape, with short wide sleeves. His night dress, which he wore beneath it, was open in front, and displayed his bony chest. A long grey beard partly concealed his sinewy neck; and on his head, which was bald, and fringed with grey curls round the sides and back, he wore a close-fitting black velvet cap. His features were bold and striking, but the eyes indicative of cunning. He had a high forehead, Roman nose, square chin, and shaggy eyebrows. Add to this description, that his bed was so placed near the narrow window that the light from it streamed in obliquely upon his remarkable figure and physiognomy, and it will readily be believed that the effect formed a study worthy of Rembrandt.

After the brief pause alluded to, the young stranger walked up to the bedside of the old man and accosted him thus :

"It is to your kind daughter, Sir, I am told, that I am indebted for most valuable services in this, my hour of need. My thanks....."

"Not another word of that, pray," replied the old man interrupting him. "Our warmest sympathy, and all that we can do for you in your heavy trouble are yours to command. But, as you see, we are poor, and...."

"Yes, I see that ; but still you can perhaps be better friends to me than you think, for some time to come. I am a perfect stranger to this place, and shall, no doubt, be detained here for many weeks. During that time your kind daughter has agreed to undertake the charge of my little one, who has been so miraculously saved. It is a comfort to me, I assure you, to think that she will be so well cared for by a lady who has contributed largely to save her life, by forethought and judicious treatment, while for several minutes she lay hovering on the verge of death. This kindness I shall never forget. For the rest—what has chanced is sad indeed—it is crushing—but it must be borne. No one was to blame for what occurred, —but *how* it happened I cannot tell. No one saw, and no one can form any idea. The only consolation is, that shocking as the misfortune is, it might have been worse still."

The old man took the hand of his young visitor, pressed it warmly, and enquired in a low tone

"Was she your wife, my poor young fellow? They tell me so?"

"Yes," replied the other briefly.

"And beautiful, I have been told," continued the old man. "You will feel her loss."

"She was a little fairy," replied the stranger, "and five years younger than myself. I had known her from childhood. We were cousins, and for some years we lived together in the same house. As children we loved each other, and our love never waxed cold. She was an angel of goodness. Oh! that I could have saved her life—but I thought that with the swimming-belt tied round her, and the line from shore attached to that, there could have been no danger. But thank Heaven, I have saved her child; and

the rest of my life I dedicate to *her*. I swear
it by the God who made me; and you, Sir,
are a witness to this vow."

"Sad, indeed!" muttered the old man, heedless
apparently of the last words which the other
had been saying. "Sad, indeed, to die so young!
But life is still before *you*—and an exciting scene
is life.   Time heals every wound, and believe
me you will live to forget this trouble, heavy
as it is. Besides, your child will remind you
of her whom you have lost, when your present
grief has subsided into a sentiment, and a
memory without a pang."

"Yes, indeed, I am glad it is a daughter; and
my earnest hope will be that she may grow up
like her mother, and love me perhaps all the
better some day for knowing that when she was
an infant I helped to save her life, by stretching
out a hand, at a time when it was a struggle to
save my own?"

"I saw it from this window, and a frightful
scene it was," replied the old man, "but poor
helpless being as I am, what could I do, except
pray idly that you might all be saved. You
struck out bravely, and have earned, I trust,

a rich reward. How old may your little darling be ?"

"About fourteen months. She was born in Malta."

"And may I ask you one more bold question?" added the old man. "Have you any valuables on board the yacht ? Anything you would greatly care to lose?"

"Some deeds and papers only. Nothing that would be of value to anyone except myself. In fact, when you sent for me just now, I was looking along the edge of the tide, for such waifs and strays from my cabin as might be washed up, and I have already found an old letter. Look."

" My daughter shall dry it for you," said the old man, " and she shall go and help you search for more."

" No, no, she has got enough on her hands already, with the child. And now, excuse me, Sir, for the present, for I must return to the shore, and keep an eye on what may be thrown up. We will have a longer chat another time. In fact, I want to ask you whether we might not save the yacht,—for both the sea and wind are going down quite fast."

At this crisis in their conversation, Jim's heavy step was heard upon the ladder; and a glance at his broad red face, as he entered the room, unceremoniously enough it is true, sufficed to show that he had recovered his good temper— to all outward appearance at least.

"You've come in the nick of time, Jim," said the old man, good-naturedly. "The gentleman was talking to me about how to save his yacht, and I was going to tell him we could manage that for him, easy enough. I was right, Jim, was I not?"

The reader shall be spared the conversation that ensued; enough that it was arranged between them that Jim was to take charge of the little vessel, and keep watch on her, and act in all matters relating thereunto, according to the suggestions and orders of old Smith, and her owner.

This having been arranged, the sailor departed; and the young stranger was about to follow him, but before doing so he approached nearer to the old man, and said, in a lower tone

"You understand, of course, my kind old friend, that all these valuable services of yours and your daughter's will be properly acknowledged by-and-bye. I have wealth wherewith to repay, as far as money can do, such obligations as you are both laying me under now."

"Another time," was the reply. "Not a word about such things at present. But let me ask you one more question. Your wardrobe, and your arrangements for the night—have you thought of those things? I see what my man has lent you, but I am afraid he may want them back, however much you may come to take a fancy to them. My own helplessness and poverty are such that I fear I can offer you no better substitute from my own outfit."

"Thank you all the same," was the reply, with a half-smile. "I have already thought about what you suggest. A boy named Joe has been sent to the nearest town for a carriage, which is to come here for me in the afternoon. In that I shall leave, in my present guise, but with such articles of apparel as we may be able to save from the wreck at low water. I shall, of course, return here early to-morrow, and in the meantime the rest of my belongings will remain under your friendly charge, and Jim's."

"We will do our best to look after them ; but may I ask you one word more ? Your name?"

" My name ? " echoed the young man in a sort of absent fit.

The querist smiled, and waited for a reply.

" My name ? Oh, I understand you. It is a very common one, and easy to remember— John Smith."

" How singular," replied the old man. " It is the same as mine. And the yacht—what may her name be, if I am not too bold to ask ? "

" The yacht's name ? Oh—the BAGATELLE."

" Of the R.T.Y.C., I think ? At least I judge so from the burgee which is still flying at the main-mast head, a yard or two above the waves."

" No, no. You are mistaken. That is some old flag that was hoisted by mistake. At this moment she does not belong to any club. I bought her in the East, and my name is not yet entered on a Club. And now, Sir, I must wish you good morning, for the present."

So saying, Mr. John Smith the younger took his leave; while Mr. John Smith the elder remained to speculate on the information he had received.

" He's a fine young fellow, certainly," he muttered to himself, " and a gentleman—there can't be a doubt of that—but—but—let us see how it all sums up. Shipping intelligence.—Wrecked on the west coast of Jersey, on the morning of June 21, 18—, the fore-and-aft schooner-yacht, BAGATELLE, belonging to no club, John Smith, Esq., owner—crew missing, and boats also—owner and a young child saved—wife rescued from the surf, but with a fractured skull. Wouldn't that sound rather odd? I fancy so. To my mind it wouldn't read exactly fair and straight,—and my own impression is, mark, that there is something wrong behind the scenes. He coloured when I asked him whether she was his wife—and he hesitated when I asked his name—and the flag produced another hitch. Jim must tell me what name is painted on her stern,—but yachts don't always carry their name outside, like traders. We must get to see her papers, anyhow. Ha, my fine young gentleman, I think I smell a rat."

Nothing of any consequence was cast ashore as the tide went down, and at noon the yacht was left high and dry upon the sands. To all appearance she had sustained no harm. Her great depth of keel had saved her. The first roller that struck her after she had touched bottom, made her heel over till her skylights and scuttle-holes were under water, and then she filled, and went down at once upon her side. She never rose again, and the seas passed over her as harmless as if she had been a pig of lead. Jim, with some men he had engaged to help him, then began their work of salvage by boring holes in her bottom to let the water from her cabins run out,—and as soon as it was practicable, the owner crawled inside to save the papers of which he had been in search. He found apparently what he looked for, in the midst of a heap of sodden and shattered relics of what were once the elegant appointments of the cabin,—and then crawled out again, and directed the men not to disturb anything inside, but to proceed at once to batten down companions, and skylights, and scuttle-holes, and caulk and pay all seams, so as to make her water-tight on deck, in order that she might rise to it, and float when the tide came up. In this job some hours were consumed ; and when the flowing tide just reached her keel once more, the carriage which had been ordered was seen standing at the cottage door.

In half-an-hour the stranded BAGATELLE was

once more afloat, and the gang of men were proceeding to warp her into deep water, and anchor her until the tide should serve for towing her into the nearest harbour they could reach that night.

"Now, my good fellows," said the owner, "you have all done your best so far, and I must leave her in your charge. If anything should go wrong, of course I sha'n't blame you. Another day I will reckon with you all for this. But it has been a sad day for me, and I can tell you I am sick at heart."

The good fellows touched their hats respectfully; and the owner walked to the carriage, got in, and was driven off.

"That's a fine young cove, ain't he?" said one of the men to Jim. "If you want a hand to tow her into harbour put *me* down for one."

And here's a dozen more of·us will join," said another. "We'd do anything for that sort of young gent—ay, if he hadn't a sou in his pocket to bless himself with. He's made of the right stuff, ain't he my lads? But don't shout. Hush! Think of the poor young cretur in the cottage yonder, with the shutters shut. It ain't often hereabouts that we see a house shut up."

CHAPTER 5.

—

AN INQUEST—A RECLUSE.

WE will not linger over the details of a sad incident. An inquest was held on the body of the deceased; and the verdict given was "accidental death." The medical evidence, however, went to show that it was not drowning which had proved fatal, but the fracture of the skull. The funeral passed off with the usual solemnity, and the mourning coach which contained the bereaved husband was followed by the majority of the male population of La Pulente, on foot. It is customary in Jersey to pay this mark of respect to the dead, and a praiseworthy custom it is. In illustration of it the writer of these lines can testify to the following fact, which came under his own knowledge not many years ago:—A skeleton of a man was thrown

up in St. Brelade's Bay, the only vestige of
clothing being a pair of heavy peasant's shoes
still firmly tied to the bones of the legs. No
one knew who the drowned man might be, or
how recently the fatal accident had occurred, but
a coffin was provided, and the remains were
decently interred, twelve of the farmers in the
neighbourhood following them to the grave. Thus
the funeral procession of the deceased young wife
of the stranger who had been cast upon that coast
included more than the above-named number of
mourners, composed of the little farmers, vraickers,
and fishermen of St. Ouen's Bay, decently attired,
each in his own suit of black; and the body was
interred in the strangers' burial ground of the
parish in which the accident occurred. In the
course of time, a neat gravestone was put up,
inscribed with the following simple words :

" In memory of ZOE, who was accidentally killed
in St. Ouen's Bay, on June 21st, 18—. She was
both a wife and a mother, and died in her eighteenth
year. This stone has been erected to her memory
by one who was present at the accident, but was
helpless to save, and who had known her from her
childhood, had loved her dearly, and will ever
deeply deplore her fate."

Weeks and months then rolled on. The child remained at La Bie, in the charge of Hannah Smith, under whose kind and fostering care it grew and prospered; and the yacht was saved, repaired, and refitted in exactly its former style; with the man Jim placed in sub-command as mate. But the owner did not remove her from the Island, except for an occasional short cruise to the neighbouring French ports; and when not in use, she remained in the harbour of St. Helier's, the Capital town, with her legs on, and her sails unbent,—which sometimes happened for months together, so that Jim led a very easy and idle life. At first her owner lived on board, as a perfect recluse, making no acquaintances whatever, and merely following his quiet hobbies of reading, sketching, and music, in a strange and solitary way; but by degrees he began to shake off these lonely habits, and took lodgings in the town, and finally gave up altogether his berth on board the yacht. It will readily be believed that these returning signs of a yearning after social life were well received in a place which is said to be one of the most dissipated in the world, and where a wealthy young widower would find but little difficulty in making friends of either sex. Once, and once only, since his arrival in the Island had he been to England, and that for but a few days, immediately after the funeral of his wife. Whenever wonder was expressed that one so young and independent should have so readily adopted Jersey as his home, his reply would be, that he had associations with the place, although painful ones, which had endeared it to him,—that his child was taken care of by people whom he liked,—that his yacht lay in a snug berth, where, in ten minutes he could be on board of her at any time,—and that he liked the Island for its own sake, and thought its scenery lovely, and its climate the most charming in the world, — besides which, all places were alike to him, as he had no profession to follow, or any coercive duties to bind him to a particular spot, and if he preferred to live in Jersey, why not? Such explanation he considered ought to be sufficient for any one to whom it might be addressed; but if not, then he had a way of silencing all further queries respecting his mode of life, by a coolness of manner which intimated pretty plainly that he had said enough.

CHAPTER 6.

THE BELL FAMILY—AN INVITATION.

Two years had elapsed since the events occurred which have been related in the preceding chapters; and again it was the height of the summer season.

In the drawing-room of a ready-furnished house, which had been taken for the summer months by its present inmates, and was cheerfully situated in a terrace commanding a view over the town of St. Helier's and St. Aubin's Bay beyond, a small family party was assembled, engaged in such occupations as were suitable to an evening without guests. Paterfamilias—who must be introduced to the reader as the Rev. Alfred Bell, was seated in an easy chair reading a copy of the *Times*, which had arrived that day from England by the mail-steamer; his wife was hurrying over the concluding pages of a new novel from Mudie's; and their daughters three, whose names were respectively, Sophy, Ellen, and Catherine — the latter a girl of seventeen, and the others older by steps of two years each—were seated at a loo table, strewn with ladies' graceful litter, and were chatting together in a low tone whilst otherwise thus engaged, viz. : Sophy was transferring sea-weeds from a dish of water in which they floated, to sheets of paper upon which they were to remain attached, and which in due time were to be bound up together in a handsome volume, which was to be presented to the Queen; Ellen was less ambitiously employed in hemming a piece of plain needlework, intended for some charitable purpose; and Kate was reading, though not so attentively as it deserves, that pretty poem, Lalla Rookh.

"Mamma," said the latter, as her mother concluded, and put down with a yawn the fashionable novel she had been reading, or rather skimming for an hour or more, " Did Sir Evelyn marry Alice at last ? "

" Of course she did, child," was the reply. "Anyone could foresee that. In novels everybody gets married at last."

" It is only in real life," said the father of the family, with a pretended sigh, and looking quizzically over the top of his newspaper, " that a man with three daughters has to calculate the extreme probability there is of their all dying old maids."

" Oh, Papa," said Kate, laughing. " I 'm sure *I* don't mean to die an old maid."

But her father took no heed of the remark, and went on reading his paper. How rude fathers are, to be sure, sometimes.

" No, my child, I don't think *you* will," said her Mamma, answering for him. " If any of you is to be an old maid it will be Sophy— for men have a wholesome dread of a blue stocking, and they are quite right. So if you 'll take my advice, my love, you 'll put away those sea-weeds, and sea-monsters that you 're so fond of, and spend more time at your piano."

" Oh, Mamma, how can you say such things of poor Sophy," retorted Kate. " Why I saw Mr. Smith, only a week ago, paying her most marked attentions, at a pic-nic."

" You little story-teller," replied her elder sister, with real, and not affected indignation. " How can *you* say such things, when you know how I hate that odious man."

"Then you're the only one who does," said Ellen. "I'm sure it's wicked of you to hate a man like that—so kind to everybody, and particularly to children."

"And so strikingly handsome," added Kate. "Who could dislike a handsome man?"

"Call *him* handsome!" said her Mamma. "What, little Smith, with his penny trumpet, and that odious yacht. *I* call him half a fool."

"But surely not *little*," said Ellen. "He's taller than Papa, and broader too,—and Papa's six feet high."

"What does a little humpty-dumpty like you, know about tall men?" replied her Mamma, not very flatteringly; but it was true that the young lady addressed was somewhat shorter than the average, and a trifle stouter too than might be thought consistent with elegance; but she had a very sweet, good face, with all the freshness and frankness of Aurora. She coloured slightly at her Mamma's remark; and her younger sister, after a short pause in the conversation, whispered chaffingly in her ear, "I know another clergyman who is a tall man too, and kind to children."

"If Mr. Smith flirts with any of us, it

certainly is not with *me*," said the eldest young lady, tossing her head disdainfully, "for if ever *I* say a thing, no matter what, he is sure to make fun of it; and I never met anyone so rude and contradictory. If I were to say to him now, it's a fine evening, he would answer at once, no it isn't, the sky is becoming overcast. I never met such a disagreeable man in my life—and what is more, I regard him as a goose."

Her Papa had now finished his leading article: so he put down the *Times*, got up, and stood with his back to the mantle-shelf, before the empty grate, prepared to take part in the conversation. It was a habit of his to stand in that way, with his hands spreading out the tails of his coat behind, while conversing with his family; and one which he had acquired in cold weather, and retained through all seasons, and to which no one ever disputed his right. He was a tall, benevolent-looking old gentleman, with curly grey hair, a slight frame, and an inelegant stoop.

"What was that you were saying about my friend Smith?" he retorted upon his eldest daughter, "that he is a goose? I deny it. I consider him a very talented young man.

Now you have *my* opinion of him. He is not only talented in all matters relating to the arts, such as painting and music, but his order of mind shows innate refinement and good breeding, —besides which he has a shrewdness and a knowledge of the world which is quite extraordinary in so young a man, and he has evidently moved in good society. I like him,—but I don't like a simpleton, or an ill-mannered brute."

"Well, Papa," the young lady replied, "all I can say is, that he does not number natural history among his accomplishments,—and that he is an idle man. His life is a useless one. But men of extraordinary talent are never idle, —they are always too ambitious for that. At least such is my conclusion from reading the lives of some really great men, in a book which you have yourself lately given me."

"But you must remember," replied her father, with the utmost courtesy, and good temper, and not in the least ruffled by the contradiction, for he had rather encouraged a spirit of argument in his eldest daughter, "You must remember that all men's natures are not alike. In some, transcendant ability shows itself quite early—for instance, Pitt was Prime Minister at twenty-three—while in others it is more slowly developed. Circumstances also may concur to call it forth early in some cases, and to retard its manifestation in others. Take the case of Buonaparte—it was by a mere chance that he was not a cab-driver in the streets of Paris."

"But still," replied his daughter, "Napoleon had distinguished himself as a mathematician when a youth, and had always shown a marked predilection for a military career."

"Then, take a better case, still," replied her father. "I have just been reading in this paper about a quiet middle-aged country gentleman in France, whom nobody had ever heard of before, but who has just made a really wonderful discovery, viz., that of fixing upon stone, or plates of metal, the fleeting images formed in the camera-obscura. His name is Niepce ; and I venture to say that it will find as honourable and as permanent a place in history as that of Napoleon, or Pitt."

"But you surely don't mean to say, Papa, that Mr. Smith is ever likely to become a Niepce ?"

"Don't be so contradictory and disagreeable, child," said her Mamma, interposing between the combatants. "If your Papa likes Mr. Smith, and thinks him a great genius, what business is that of ours?"

"No, no,—don't scold her," said her Father. "What she said was quite to the purpose, and I'm not at all sure she hadn't the best of the argument."

There was a pause after this, and then the second daughter said timidly, "I don't know whether Mr. Smith is clever or not, but I'm sure he is a very kind man, and never intentionally rude to anyone. See how fond he is of his little daughter, and how he romps with her, and tosses her about. I'm sure he never goes over to La Pulente to see her, without a quantity of sweetmeats and toys,—and what a lovely little creature she is, and so fond of him too."

"But not in the least like him in face," said the youngest sister, "though they've both got magnificent eyes; besides, he is very tall, and I think she seems to be short for her age."

"I have not yet seen her," said the Papa. "That is a treat to come. But I've seen several portraits of her, for his rooms are hung all over with his own pretty sketches of her in charcoal and red chalk. He knocks off one of these in a couple of hours, and very masterly they are, I can tell you. I wish he would do one for me of my own little pet," and as he said it, he looked archly at his youngest daughter, until the colour began to mantle on her cheek.

" Why, you monkey," said her Mamma, " You have been flirting with him already—I know you have. You are blushing, child,—I declare you are."

At this rebuke, the poor girl absolutely put her hands before her face ; and they all laughed immensely at her—but her father the most.

" I heard him say once," he remarked, " that he liked young things, and that if he were ever to have the choice of a wife from a family of daughters, it would be odds but he took the youngest. Come here, my youngest one,—confess now,—what has he been saying to you, Eh ? Tell me, like a good girl. I 'll keep it a secret— I will indeed."

" Oh, Papa,—nothing at all, I assure you."

" No, no,—that won't do for me. I know he has. Come here, now. I must and will have it out of you."

" He asked her, only yesterday, Papa," said

Ellen, laughing, " to let him paint her portrait.
I heard it myself, and I vouch for the fact."

" Gracious goodness," said their mother, "what
next, I should like to know ? Why, I 've heard
that he has been for two months, or more,
painting that horrid bold creature, Eliza Kemp;
and his housekeeper told me that the picture
is now hanging over his mantel-shelf, and that
he made her take down the pier glass to make
way for it, because he said he liked to see *her*
face there better than his own. Her great
vulgar staring eyes seem to follow you all
about the room. I told Mrs. Brown to turn
it with its face to the wall every time he
went out, and to let him see it so when he came
in again."

" It 's not a bad picture though," said Mr. Bell.
" I 've seen it, and I consider myself rather a
judge. She 's a fine creature, that girl, even if
she is a lump of vulgarity,—and he has idealized
her, and made quite a Juno of her. As for his
offer to paint my Katie, if that 's really true,
I 'm sure I don't see why not, if I go with her.
I should like a portrait of her immensely, and
she 'd make a perfect Flora—wouldn't she ? "
and as he said it, he pulled her towards him,

and put his arm kindly round her waist, and gave her forehead a loving kiss.

" Well, I don't know what *some* men are made of," said the Mamma. " I dare say you 'd let him paint *me*, if he were to ask. Wouldn't you now? I 'll be bound you would."

" We won't discuss that possible contingency, my love," was the reply. " Suppose we drop the conversation. Go and give us some music, girls, before I 'm off to the Club."

But it happened that the conversation about Mr. Smith—whom the reader has already perceived to be the owner of the BAGATELLE—was not to be brought to a close so suddenly, for no sooner had Sophy and Ellen seated themselves at the piano, to perform a duet, than a maid-servant entered the room and put into their father's hand a note, which she said had been brought by a sailor man, who was to wait for a reply.

" What's all this about? " said Mr. Bell, running his eye hastily over the contents. " Oh, show the man into the kitchen, Betsy, and give him a glass of ale. I 'll just talk this matter over with your mistress, and send him down a note to take back."

He then added, when the girl had left,

"Why this note is from Smith himself. They say, talk of the old gentleman and he shows himself, and this is something like it. He invites us all to go out in the BAGATELLE, for a sail in the Bay, and luncheon afterwards within the harbour, the day after to-morrow—and to meet some mutual friends. What say you, girls?"

"Oh, how delightful," half screamed the young lady of seventeen, answering for the whole party, and in her eagerness almost snatching the note from her father's hand, in order that she might read it for herself. Very rude indeed, but she was the spoilt child, that same Katie— as youngest daughters often are by their good Papas.

"Come, read it out," said her mother, "don't keep it all to yourself, child—we want to hear." So the young lady read as follows, with a sparkle in her eye, and a flush upon her cheek.

"*The* BAGATELLE, *Wednesday, June* 19.

"Mr. Smith presents his compliments to Mrs. and the Rev. Alfred Bell, and their daughters, and will feel much pleasure if they will join him, and a few mutual friends, for a sail in the Bay in his little yacht, the day after to-morrow,—the sail to be followed by a luncheon on board, within the harbour. Weather permitting, of course, so far as the sail is concerned. To meet at the harbour-slip at ten—not later, on account of the tide."

"Oh, won't it be nice?" said the gleeful girl, handing the note to her Mamma, and never for a moment doubting that the rest would view the invitation in the same light as she did herself. And, in fact, they did all look pleased, even Sophy herself, notwithstanding her previous remarks in disparagement of the writer of the note.

"It is certainly very kind of him to think of us," said the Mamma, "and I really don't see why we shouldn't accept, although we know but little of him at present. He is often giving these luncheons on board his yacht this season, and people say they're very nice and *distingués* indeed. I thought some day he might be inviting us to one."

"But stop a bit," said Papa. "We mustn't all go—that would be bad taste. You can fancy how small the cabin is. Ten are quite enough to fill it, and if we go five strong, I'm sure he would think it a mistake. Two, or at most, three of us, would be quite enough. Suppose

I accept for myself and one of my daughters—that will look the best—and no doubt the turn will come for Mamma and the others another time."

Ellen was the first to acquiesce in her Papa's proposal that some of them should stand out. "I'll be one, Papa, to give up," she said.

Her elder sister was bound to follow suit, if only for the sake of consistency; and their Mamma added

"Well, I hate the water, so Papa shall go with Kate."

This being arranged to the satisfaction of all parties—at least so far as appearance went—the Reverend Papa adjourned to his study, and wrote the following reply to the note of invitation which he had received :—

"My dear Smith,—It is very kind of you to ask us all to join you in a sail in your pretty Bagatelle on Friday, but we fear that five of us would be crowding your cabin too much—particularly as you talk of inviting other friends. We have arranged therefore that I will accept for myself and my youngest daughter only,—if that is quite agreeable to you.

"Very faithfully yours,

"Alfred Bell."

The note was handed to our old friend Jim; and the parson returned to the drawing-room, and repeated its contents, adding

"I am not sure whether it is very wise of me, though, to introduce him up here,—for of course, after this we shall have to include him in our circle of friends, and return his kindness in some way. It was not exactly etiquette of him either, to invite us, now I think of it; for although he and I are pretty intimate at the Club, yet he' knows but little of any of you, and has never been formally introduced to you by me. He ought by rights to have waited until I had made the first advance. However, I suppose etiquette need not be very strictly observed in a place like this, where we are only visitors for a time, and where intimacies can easily be shaken off, and need not extend to our own home when we get back. Still, it is one thing to be friends with a pleasant fellow whom you may happen to meet at a club at a watering place, and even to like him immensely as a companion to yourself, but another thing to introduce him to your wife and daughters. One can't be too particular; and now I think of it people do whisper strange things about him."

"Oh Papa, how can you talk in that way?" said the much-indulged Kate. "What a perfect gentleman he is. I'm sure no one should say a word against him to *me*, if *I* were ever to call myself his friend." And having delivered herself of the above spirited sentiment, with a blush a second time mantling to her cheek, she darted from under her long lashes a beam of reproach into her father's face.

"Much *you* know about these things, Miss," was the reply. "People do talk about him, there's no doubt; and they think it odd that he never seems to know anyone in England, and that he avoids so systematically as he does, all allusion to any kith or kin, except his little daughter; and I have certainly noticed how proud and supercilious he can be, when chaffed about himself. He has not a good temper, I fancy; in fact I'm sure he has not."

"Oh, Papa," said Ellen, "what a shame!"

"Well, I grant you there is much in his favour too," continued her Papa, "or *I* should never have become so thick with him as I am. For instance, he never gambles, and has no low tastes. I believe he smokes, but not much,—and he certainly doesn't drink. His tastes are all rational and intellectual, and he has talent, beyond a doubt. He seems to have plenty of money, yet is not extravagant ; and he pays his way punctually, and never gets in debt,—at least so they say. Mrs. Brown swears by him, and says he's the model lodger—the best she ever had. Then, in his person, he is neat and gentlemanly, without being a fop ; and all the college boys like him, for he goes down with them to bathe, and plays cricket and football with them, and that sort of thing, and tips them when they do well. All this is greatly in his favour ; and upon my word I don't know what you can say for a man more than this. For my own part, I like him ; and I don't see a bit why we shouldn't all know him, and ask him up."

Thus the worthy Rector conciliated his conscience, and stifled a scruple which some people might think overstrained.

CHAPTER 7.

—

TRAITS OF CHARACTER.

FROM the conversation recorded in the preceding Chapter the reader will have caught a glimpse of the mode of life and tastes of the owner of the BAGATELLE at that time—that is to say after he had been in Jersey two years. He lived in comfortable well-appointed lodgings, he kept his yacht at the pier, he was beginning to mix in the best society of the island, and he amused himself with painting and sketching, in which arts he appeared to possess something far beyond mere amateur proficiency. He was tall and strikingly handsome in person, a gentleman in manners and appearance, and apparently well off. To this must now be added that he made no secret of his continued regard for his old friends at La Pulente. And yet it need not be thought strange that he should feel attached to them, when it is remembered that they had befriended him in a great trouble, and were people of education who, although poor then, had seen better days. Thus, his little daughter, Mabel by name, remained in Hannah's charge, and he went over to see her, and gossip with the old man at least once in every week. Nor were these visits to St. Ouen's Bay by any means unentertaining ones; for old Smith, the bedridden hermit, lying on his ottoman by the side of his little window, in his strangely-appointed attic, was a profound original in his way. Before the accident happened which had cost him the use of his legs, he had travelled a good deal, had been to sea, had made money in a variety of ways and lost it again, had been a smuggler, a lawyer, a doctor, a ship-broker, and heaven knows what; besides which he had read, and reflected much after a fashion of his own; and had earned money by contributions to newspapers and magazines. He had also a rich and racy talent in conversation, with just so much laxity of moral tone as to render his anecdotes *piquants* and diverting. It is not wonderful, therefore, that his young namesake should have continued to visit him, or have come to regard him with some sort of liking, if not with esteem.

But the reader may be inclined to ask why little Mabel was left in the charge of such strange people, and in such an outlandish place; and why her Papa did not let her live with him in the town, where she could have had a proper nurse, or governess, and other children to play with?

The reply is simple enough. On the one hand, nothing could induce Old Smith to remove his quarters from La Bie; while, on the other hand, nothing could induce young Smith to remove Mabel from Hannah's charge. That is why he left her where she was. Once, when the old man was hard pressed by him to give up his homely quarters in St. Ouen's Bay, and remove from his attic to a more comfortable bedroom in the town, he replied with much energy and animation

"My good fellow, you don't understand my idiosyncrasy at all. You think that because I lie here inactive, from day to day, and year to year, that therefore I must be dull, and want society. It is no such thing. I am by nature an unsocial being, and my chief enjoyment in life is to lie and watch a view from my window, over some grand solitude like this Bay. The love of grand scenery has always been a passion of mine, and a view a necessity of life. I can't live without it. You, who are an artist, ought to understand this. Now, look through my little pane, and tell me what you could show me in your town to compare with that great Western ocean, which I have only to raise my head to see at any time, in calm or gale, in sunshine or shadow, in moonlight or starlight, at sunrise or sunset? Why, dingy brick houses, and streets full of people whose occupations would not amuse me in the least. What now, do you suppose, is the real event of the day to me, as I lie here? I'll be bound you think, to read the latest copy of the *Times* that you bring me,—or to watch the mail boat pass, and note exactly the hour of her arrival, and speculate on the news she brings. Not a bit. My great event of every day is the sunset over yonder sea. Then I build my castles in the air, and grow young again—for my mind and fancy are young yet, quite as young as ever. Now, what could you give me in the town to compare with such a sight as that, which, even if I could see it there at all, would have its exquisite illusions and fairy visions disturbed by the jarring sounds and sights of a civilization which does not greatly concern myself, and which seems to get uglier with every fresh step it takes, and to be the antagonistic element of beauty in the world. What I should lose by a removal to the town would be the greatest delight I have in life; while I should gain, what? You tell me I should oftener get a change of books— but what are books to me? — other men's thoughts—while for the most part I prefer my own. And then, as to visitors and gossiping friends—they would only bore me — for there would be no sympathy between us, and *I* should have to amuse *them*. No. I prefer to live in this wild spot, and so does Hannah too. I may not have many years to live—perhaps not many months, or even weeks—but my earnest prayer is that I may be left to die in this place in peace, on some calm evening, when I may breathe forth my last sigh alone, and lying here, as the sun goes down upon the sea. To disturb me now would be to kill me outright, by robbing me of the last joy I have on earth—the poetry of nature—the sights and the sounds of this wild coast. No, my friend. Through your kindness, this little cottage has been rendered as comfortable to us as it can be, and all the cares of life have been removed. Come here then, and gossip with the old man when you like, and as often as you like, and the oftener the better, but never, again allude to the possibility of my removing from this place. You don't understand my idiosyncrasy. The love of nature has been a passion with me all my life, and therefore my bane when it was not gratified; besides which, I am an unsocial being, because I have never found anyone constituted like myself."

"But the child must be a trouble to you, my dear Sir. Its endless noise and boisterous spirits, which no one can control, must worry you—I know they must."

"No—there you're wrong again. Hav' n't I told you a hundred times that I love that little darling more than I can express. She is like a ray of sunshine in the house. If you ever dare to take her from me—mind—I'll be revenged— and that I could be, in a way you little think."

"I dare say you could," replied the other, laughing.

"Don't tempt me — that's all. If you ever dare to take away my little pet, before I'm taken away myself, feet foremost, I'll—I won't say what."

"Well then, she shall stay another year with you, at any rate. I am quite content; and when she does leave you, it shall be only her noise and worry that you shall miss. This I promise you—do you understand?"

"Never mind. Speak no more about it. Hand me your books and papers. What's the best news to-day? There, — leave me now, and go and romp with her, and make the most noise you can, for I love to hear it. It's the next best music to the sea."

Then the old man would bury himself in the batch of news; for notwithstanding all that he had said about the sunset, and the poetry of nature, and the sights and sounds of that wild coast, he loved dearly, helpless as he was and solitary, to con over the news from England, and was even better posted in it, so far as the date of his last newspaper went, than many an active citizen of the great Babylon itself. The sequel will show, moreover, that the true character of this old man was difficult to fathom, even by a deep sea lead.

As for little Mabel, then three years old, she seemed likely to prove a character too, as she grew up. Her animal spirits were unbounded, and quite beyond Hannah's control; and she looked the picture of rosy and exuberant health. Her great delight was to toddle down to the sea beach, and dabble in the pools amongst the rocks, and scream with a child's ecstacy as she watched the gambols of the shrimps and little fish; or decked herself with long fronds of seaweed, and clambered up to the attic, and teazed "old Jack" with them—as he had taught her to call him. She was not exactly a pretty child, although she had fine hazel eyes, and an abundance of wavy brown curls; but her face was expressive of every transient feeling of an impulsive nature, and with the beauty which perfect health always adds to youth. She was small for her age, but seemed to have inherited much of her mother's grace. On the whole she was a loveable and amusing child, and a favourite with all who knew her, both old and young.

The reader has now been fairly introduced to

the two Smiths and little Mabel; but first impressions are often erroneous, and no person's character can be thoroughly understood until it has been tested by some ordeal in which the amount of selfishness, which is more or less inherent in every human being as a motive or guiding principle of action, is correctly ascertained in its relation to other influences. It is just possible that first impressions may be wrong in the present case, and that a further revelation of character, as regards the two men, to be made in the next chapter, may prove a surprise. Moreover the reader must be reminded, before proceeding further with the tale, of certain suspicions which old Smith had formed respecting his young namesake, on the day when they first became acquainted. During the two years which had since elapsed, the mind of the old man had never ceased to brood over those suspicions; and with an inherent meanness of disposition, and love of dark romance and intrigue, he had been ever on the watch, with cat-like patience and fox-like cunning, for such further light as chance might throw upon what had become deeply and personally interesting to him to discover, viz.: the antecedents of the

owner of the BAGATELLE.　The sequel will show
that chance had been singularly propitious on
many occasions in helping him to a solution
of an enigma which had engrossed his thoughts ;
and that at length, in his opinion, the time
for turning his knowledge to his own advantage
had actually arrived.

CHAPTER 8.

ANGRY WORDS.—SUSPICIONS CONFIRMED.

On the day preceding that which had been fixed for the sail and pic-nic in the BAGATELLE, her owner had an altercation with his man Jim, whom long idleness had rendered independent and saucy; and this, in connexion with other circumstances about to be described, led to a far more serious quarrel with the old man at La Bie. How all this happened, we shall now proceed to tell.

On the day in question, young Smith was seen, shortly after leaving his yacht, driving in a hired horse and gig at a great pace, in the direction of La Pulente. There was a cloud upon his brow, and anger in his eye, and anyone could see at a glance that his temper had been severely ruffled that morning. On arriving at the cottage where his old namesake dwelt, he put up his steaming horse in the outhouse at the back; and then, not finding either Hannah or Mabel in either of the lower rooms, mounted at once to the attic, and presented himself, in the worst possible humour, at the bedside of the old man.

"You are an unexpected visitor this morning," said the latter, sitting up to receive his guest. "I did not think to see you over until Sunday. Nothing wrong has happened, I trust, to put you out of sorts — for you look as black as the old father of mischief himself?"

"I am sorry to say that something *has* occurred to vex me," was the reply, "and I have driven over to-day to be the first to tell you of it — for Jim will give you his version of the affair, no doubt. You know that his conduct to me for some time past has not been so respectful as I like, and I have had to complain to you about it; but this morning he has thought fit to break out into open mutiny, and defy me. What he said I shall not repeat, but it was something which I don't quite understand, and don't mean to put up with either. He was half drunk at the time, or I verily believe I should have given him in charge of the *Centenier*. As it is, he has simply had notice to quit my service in a week. I am not one to stand much cheek from a man to whom I have been so uniformly kind and indulgent as I have to him, and who has led a nearly idle life at my expense for two years."

"Ha!" replied the old man, fixing his expressive grey eyes keenly upon his visitor. "Have you and Jim quarrelled at last? I thought it would come to that some day. I suppose he has been reading the *Times* paper lately, instead of minding his work."

This was said with a marked expression of irony and defiance, and it had by no means a mollifying effect upon the other—who replied

"I have no conception what you mean, Sir,—or what Jim meant either; but this I can tell you, that I am not one to brook any impudence, either from him or you, and that if you back him in his improper conduct to me, our connexion will cease too. I shall settle with you, and take my child away at once."

"Whew," whistled the old man contemptuously. "Don't you know, Sir, that Jim is a very particular protégé of mine, and that you must not dismiss him from your service, unless I choose—or take away the child either?"

"Pooh — you forget yourself, Sir," was the reply. " What power have you, I should like to know, over my actions ? How can you prevent my doing as I please, either in the matter of Jim, or of little Mabel ? If you suppose I will submit to be dictated to by you, or by any man living, you are egregiously mistaken in my character. I have merely come over now to tell you what *has* occurred, and what I have actually *done*, in order that you might hear it first from me—not to ask your advice in the matter. I now wish you good morning, Sir ; and when your account against me is made out, you will know where to send it — although, now I think of it, the balance will be in my favour, as I have always paid you in advance."

So saying, he was about to leave the room in a towering passion, and had actually put his hand upon the door, when the old man called him back, in a tone as proud and resolute as his own.

" Henry Clifford," he said, " I command you to return to my bedside, and listen to what I have got to tell you, and propose to you for your own safety ; for know that both your life and your property are in my power."

At the sound of that name, Henry Clifford,

the young man started as if a thunderbolt had fallen at his feet; and his cheek lost at once its crimson hue of passion. For a full minute he remained motionless, with his hand upon the door latch; and then he returned to the bedside of the old man.

"What is it that you know about me?" he asked, in accents of ill-suppressed emotion.

"Much," was the cool reply. "Just so much as to place you completely in my power. If you dare to take away that child, or attempt to leave this island without my full knowledge and consent, the Sheriff of St. Helier's shall lay his hand upon your collar and lodge you in the town jail—and that without any other warrant than a word from me, which could be conveyed to him by letter, in an hour, from this place. Jerseymen know how to make laws in their own defence, and if strangers think them oppressive they should keep away. You are in my power, Henry Clifford. Now, what have you got to say?"

There was again a pause for a full minute; and then the old man put his hand beneath his pillow, and drew out a pistol, which he cocked, saying at the same time

"I may be an old bedridden, abject, helpless thing, but I have still strength enough left to pull a trigger, and eyesight enough to take deadly aim. That menacing glance of yours, Mr. Clifford, will avail nothing."

"Pooh," replied the young man, with recovered composure and *hauteur*. "My glance was one of contempt—not of menace. You mistake me most absurdly, through your own foolish fears. I menace no one with personal violence who does not first threaten me with the same— but most assuredly not a helpless old being like you. Put that thing away at once. I have simply come back to your bedside to hear what it is that you profess to know about me, as well as to ascertain the sources of your information, and the meaning of your threats."

The old man uncocked his weapon, and put it back, saying in a milder tone

"We are both fools to quarrel, and lose our temper. Our interests are the same, and we must try and pull together. I had a great deal to talk over with you calmly, had you come on Sunday; but you have forestalled it by coming here so suddenly to-day, and aggravating me with that story of your silly altercation with Jim. Suppose you leave me for an hour, and take a walk upon the beach; then return, and I will discuss with you calmly what I have got to say. We are both too excited now to continue this conversation in a style which will lead to any good. Believe me, I do not want to break with you, but rather to act as your counseller and your friend. There—go now —and leave me to myself for the time I said."

The young man, somewhat softened and reassured, complied with this request, and took a stroll upon the beach.

The hour of suspense was over at last, and he returned to the cottage. He met Hannah and little Mabel at the door. The latter did not bound up into his arms with her usual glee, but looked at him timidly, and turned away her face—for there was an unwonted expression in his own that frightened her. He tapped her kindly on the neck, and passed on. To Hannah he did not say a word.

The old man was waiting to receive him, with a clear and open brow. All traces of the late quarrel had passed off. He was the first to speak. He said

" Sit down, Mr. Clifford, by my side upon the bed. We must have a long talk, and I must tell you what I know about you, and make you a definite proposition also. I will come quickly to the point, and will not keep you in suspense. It is important to us both that we should understand each other fully. Now your account of yourself is this : that your name is John Smith—that the yacht's name is the BAGATELLE—that she belongs to you—that the young creature who perished in the surf was your wife, Zoe by name—and that the child whom you saved, with Hannah's help, is your daughter Mabel. But I have learnt a very different story. It is, that your name is Henry Clifford—that the yacht's name is the LURLINE—that she does not rightly belong to you—that Zoe was not your wife, but the wife of one Charles Marsden—and that Mabel is not your daughter, but his. What have you to say to this ? Is your story, or mine, the true one ? "

" May I ask where you learnt all these particulars respecting me ? " replied the young man, evasively.

" By all means. Ask what you like, and I will answer it."

" Then how did you learn that my name is Henry Clifford, and not John Smith ? "

" I saw it written on the fly leaf of a book which you once lent me."

" And how did you learn about Marsden, and Zoe, and Mabel, and the LURLINE ? "

" From a letter which Jim found in the pocket of his overalls, which you wore on the day of the wreck. Here it is. Read it," said the old man, handing him the letter.

It was written upon thin Foreign paper—was much discoloured by sea water, and half effaced—but was legibly addressed to Charles Marsden, Esq., Lurline Yacht, Nice. The first few sentences, which were all, except the signature and a short postcript, that could be clearly made out, ran thus

" London, April 20, 18—.

" MY DEAR CHARLES,—I 've got lots of news for you about my precious self, and your old pals, but first let me congratulate you on your own sublime good luck. I heard it through the 'fiddler.' It is most refreshing to the mind. It falls like rain upon the parched sand. So the old cock is dead at last, and your pretty Zoe entitled to the interest of £15,000 during her life, and the principal to come to little Mabel at her death. Let me see. Mabel is now a year old; and that detested Harry Clifford is executor to the will.

" Your idea, of course, is grand, if you can only carry it...."

The rest of the letter was effaced, all but the name of the writer, and an unimportant postscript at the end.

When he had read it, the young man returned it, and said

" But how did you know that the name of my yacht was the LURLINE?"

" Jim told me that. The name is carved upon one of the beams of the forecastle."

" And is this all the wonderful evidence you have against me, Sir?" demanded the young man, with a contemptuous smile.

" Not quite. Observe," was the reply, " that the letter is signed Jeremiah Stubbs. Now, whether that was a mere *nom de plume*, or the real name of the writer, matters not. Suppose I tell you that I have advertised in the *Times*, thus. If Jeremiah Stubbs, who addressed a letter, dated London, April 20, 18—, to Charles Marsden Esq., Lurline Yacht, Nice, will communicate with so-and-so, he will hear of something to his advantage; and if I tell you besides, that this advertisement *has* met with a satisfactory reply, what will you say then?"

" Simply that you are a deceitful and ungrateful old villain—that is all—an old reptile who deserves to be stamped out."

" Delicious," cried the old man, rubbing his hands with glee. "I suppose now, Mr. Clifford, I have told you quite enough. You won't want to hear any more. But stop a bit. Wait till I pay you the balance of your account. Then you may take the child away, and be off. We will give you a week's start of us, if only for a better chase."

There was a pause again, during which each of them looked sternly in the other's face. At length the young man said, with calmness, but with deep reproach

" I did not deserve this from you, Sir. Whatever may have been my crime—or I should rather say my blunder, for it was not a crime—I have been more than kind and generous to you and Hannah. But denounce me, if you choose. I promise you there shall be no chase. I am not a hare, or a fox, to run for dear life at the first baying of the hounds. I shall take away the child from you to-day, and wait where all the world can find me. Then, if it should be proved against me that I have really broken the strict letter of the law, I will tell my own tale truly, and let people condemn me or not, as they think fit. It is enough for me to know that I acted unselfishly, and as I thought for the best, in a way that my conscience approved. I wish you good morning, vile old man, and I leave you to do your worst. I defy you, and I spit upon you with contempt."

"Hush!" said the other. "You and I are fools to quarrel, for our interests are now the same. You can make it worth my while to shield you; and I can do so effectually, if you will only follow my advice. Let us not insult and irritate each other. Let us be friends. Have I not kept your secret inviolate for two years? Why then should I divulge it now? I offer you my hand. Forget what I have said. Go and romp with the little one again, and let us be as happy as we were before. I am sorry I said what I did, but you provoked me to it. You have nothing to fear from me or Jim, so long as you let things go on as I wish; but you must give him work, and stop his drink. He has not had half enough to do."

To this offer of renewed friendship, couched in the very blandest tones, the young man made no reply, but sat down upon the bed, and rested his head upon his hand, as if in a train of painful thought. At length he said—raising his eyes and fixing them sternly upon his companion

"You told me, Sir, just now, that my *life* as well as my property was in your power. What did you mean by that? Am I to understand that you, or any other persons, suspect me of foul play towards poor Zoe? You must and shall answer me this question truly, and on your oath."

"I will, then, most willingly and gladly," was the reply. "I swear to you that if for a moment I did conceive it possible that you might have struck her on the head with a marlinspike, or some such implement, as she was struggling after her fall into the sea, yet that I abandoned the suspicion at once, as quite improbable and absurd. No one who saw you, as I did through my glass, behave so gallantly in rescuing the young child,

could suppose for a moment that you had
murdered that child's mother but an instant
before.   Such an idea would be scouted even
in the wildest romance.   I think the probability
is that the poor young creature fell backwards,
when that heavy roller rushed against her
as she stood upon the rail, and that she
struck her head against the channel as she
fell into the sea.   That I swear to you is
my belief—and always has been."

" Then why did you dare to hint at something
worse ? However, I breathe more freely now.
The rest can be explained. I have been guilty
of no act of fraud — as little Mabel shall
herself admit one day, when she is old enough
to understand my recital of what occurred
on board the yacht, and since. My conduct,
I grant, may have been peculiar, and I may
have taken the law into my own hand; but I
distinctly deny having committed any intentional
act of fraud, or having acted with any but the
very best intentions towards her."

" My poor lad," replied the old man, offering
him a second time the hand of reconciliation,
" I know that what you say is true. I believe
it firmly, and would maintain it against the

world. I have read your character through and through, and I have never met a man in whose integrity I would place more faith than I would in yours. No doubt the temptation to what you did was great, and you acted as you thought was best; but I must tell you that there are now two parties to be consulted before your plans can be carried out—and that I am one. I hold the sword of Damocles above your head; but I promise you that the hair by which it hangs shall not snap in my hands, so long as you consult me, and follow in all things my advice. My terms are easy ones, I promise you. Agree to them, and you shall be safe. Do you consent"?

The young man smiled, and shook his head.

" Then you think me an old rogue, presuming on the hold I have got over you to act the tyrant and extortioner, Eh? But I will prove to you that I am in truth your friend, and that you will find me one, as long as you remain one to yourself. Listen. When you first knew me, I was in the hard gripe of poverty. True, I had bought this desolate hut, in *quartiers*, as they call it here, by paying one third of its price, or thereabouts, in money, and saddling myself with the rest in *rentes*; but bedridden and helpless as I am, I had then but little left—in fact only just so much to live upon as I could contrive to earn as I lay here, by the use of my brains and pen. How we managed for two years to make a wretched income, and eke it out, does not matter now, for that trial has been passed, and with it passed away also the temptation to evil, and the curse of want. You came — thrown up like a blessing to us by the waves — and you placed the child in our care, and paid us so handsomely for her support as to supply our every want. Then followed rest to me from the grinding worry of earning a wretched income as I lay here; and the multitude of little comforts which you heaped upon us with a generosity that you little thought was so well repaid by me—for I have known your secret from the very first. All this generosity I liked you for; and by degrees I came to love the child. With my altered circumstances I became an altered man, and a better man; and I wish now to be your friend if you will let me. Do you take my hint?"

" Plainly then, I do not," was the somewhat stern reply. " What you say sounds plausible enough, but I have sufficient knowledge of the human face to perceive in yours a crafty expression which belies your words. You are keeping something back."

"All in good time, " replied the other. " You have had a fox to deal with, no doubt; but you have gained in that wise old fox a partner in your scheme—and it is lucky for you that you have. Henceforth, then, let us pull together. Shall I tell you what I have proposed? It is that you shall be the sleeping partner, and I the active one. Do you agree to that ? "

" Positively, Sir, I don't understand you in the least."

" Pooh ! " said the old man, pettishly. "Then I won't waste any more of my precious words upon you. Pay me down a thousand pounds or I will betray your secret at once."

" I thought it was coming to that," replied the young man, contemptuously. " You want me to bribe you handsomely, to hold your tongue. But suppose I tell you that your surmises about me are so indefinite as not to be worth my notice; and that the scraps of evidence which you have collected are insufficient to form just grounds for my arrest. What then? What does your wonderful evidence amount to after all? An old letter, half-effaced; a word carved upon a beam; and a name written upon the fly-leaf of a book! It is too absurd."

"But you forget," said the old man, "how strong the circumstantial evidence against you is, which that letter supplies."

"And *you* forget too, old fox," replied the other, "how easily I can snatch it from you, and destroy it on the spot."

And with the rapidity of thought, as he said this, he seized the old man's wrists in his iron grip, and whilst he held them tight in one hand, he removed the letter, and the pistol also, from beneath the pillow with the other, adding

"Palavering old fool, I shall now leave you to do your worst. Consult with Jeremiah Stubbs, and take any course you like. I know you now for the most ungrateful, the most lying, and the meanest old hypocrite on earth, and I shall act accordingly, without any scruple, in my own defence."

He left the room, descended the step-ladder quickly, and went out. Five minutes after, the old man heard him drive away at a swift pace.

CHAPTER 9.

—

AN ADVERTISEMENT.

THE sound of wheels had scarcely died away, when Hannah, who had heard from her own room the altercation in the attic, went to her father's side. She was in tears, and trembling, and there was a look of deep anxiety as well as of reproach in her good honest face.

"This is how things always end with us," she said. "My father, experience will never make you wise. It is the same old story over and over again. You are always plotting and scheming, and knowing more than your neighbours, and thinking to outwit people who are kind to you, and doing you all the good they can. See how happy we have been for the last two years; and now we shall be destitute and in misery again, because you could not let well

N

alone. That horrid advertisement that you saw
a week ago seems to have turned your brain,
and made an altered man of you. What
insane folly it is. What business have you
with other people's affairs ? What good can an
old helpless man like you do, by intermeddling ?
You can only bring misery by it on yourself
and me. Now you have offended that most
kind and excellent young man, who has been
an angel of goodness to us, and we shall see
no more of him, or his bank notes either. It
is the same old story, over and over again—
always squabbling and acting meanly, and never
content. Here we are, left destitute again !"

"Hush, my child,—and don't torment me
in my trouble," replied her father. "When
a man is down, some woman that is dear to
him, or ought to be, is always sure to come
and kick him. I did the best I could. I kept
bad temper down. I tried to mollify him.
Twice I offered him my hand, which he refused.
He is an intractable young bull—or rather a
wild hyæna, whom it is impossible to tame by
any arts. A more hot-headed young fool I
never came across. But then, it is true, he
did not know of this advertisement, which

appeared in the *Times* a fortnight since. He brought me himself the very paper that it was in—the idiot. Here girl, read it, and see what you can make of it ; and when you have read it, advise me what to do."

So saying, he handed her the copy of the *Times*, in the second column of which the following advertisement had appeared :—

£100 REWARD!

TO anyone who will give true information respecting the fate of the yacht Lurline, a schooner of 28 tons, N.M., which was deserted by her crew on the night of June 19th, 18—, off the Wolf Rock, near the Land's End ; and also of a lady and her infant child, who remained on board, and whose names are respectively Zoe and Mabel Marsden. The same reward will also be given to anyone who will supply such information as shall lead to the conviction of a young man, 24 years of age, named Henry Clifford, who is known to have embezzled and diverted to his own use the property of Charles Marsden, husband of the aforesaid Zoe, and who is still alive. Address to Charles Marsden, Albion Coffee House, Southampton.

" Well, Hannah, what do you think of that ?" asked the old man, as soon as she had read it over twice.

"Who is Henry Clifford? And what yacht is meant by the LURLINE?" she enquired.

"Henry Clifford, *alias* John Smith, is a person whom you know well; and the LURLINE, *alias* the BAGATELLE, is a yacht which you have seen, Hannah. Now do you understand?"

"Are you sure of this?"

"There cannot be a doubt. See, here is the name Henry Clifford, at full, written on a fly leaf of a book that he lent me,—and Jim has seen the name LURLINE carved upon a beam above his berth. Besides, was it not a Zoe who was brought dead into this house,—and is not her child's name Mabel? The date of the desertion of the vessel by her crew also agrees exactly with that of the day when she was cast ashore at our very feet. There cannot be a doubt at all about who is who, and what is what. The only question is, what course are we now to follow? Let your woman's instinct guide me to a right decision. Before us now are destitution, and the workhouse; but, on the other hand, I may gain £100 reward."

"By betraying one who has been so kind to us, and causing him to be transported, for life? Oh, never! We cannot be so mean."

"But think, Hannah, of an only child severed from its true parent; and he, perhaps, himself in need."

"That is shocking too! Who could have thought that a youth so kind and good, apparently, could have done this wicked thing! But why has the father waited all this time? Why did he not advertise before?"

"That is odd, certainly," replied the old man. "But I think it can be explained thus. He was on board the yacht during the gale, and may have left her in the boat along with the crew. They may have been picked up by an outward bound vessel, and taken to the world's end; and he may have had to wait for months in an outlandish place, without money and without friends, and then have received information that his property had been seized, and his child taken off, and have had to endure hardships and poverty on his tedious return home. He may have reached England a beggar and in rags—who can say? The picture I draw is not a fanciful one—it is most probably quite true."

"But what does the unhappy youth himself say?" enquired Hannah, "for I heard angry words between you both just now?"

"I have not shown him this advertisement. I reserved that heaviest *coup* of all for the last; but he was off before I had the chance to say a word about it. He has no conception that Mabel's father is still alive. If he had, I dare say he would return the money. The man, I fancy, was a scamp; and Clifford, for fear that Mabel's money should be dissipated, is holding it in trust for her. He told me that he and Zoe were cousins. That, I think, is how the matter stands; but mind, it is only my suspicion. Young Clifford is a violent, passionate man, but warm-hearted, and not dishonourable. Still, he has broken the law, and put himself in jeopardy. I had hoped to be his friend, and to have screened him effectually while he worked out his own good intentions; but I asked him for a material guarantee for the payment for my services, and at the bare mention of the thing he flew into a rage, insulted me, and took himself off. Now then, my daughter, what are we to do? There is nothing but destitution before us, since we are no longer to be supported by him. Shall we go to the workhouse—or do something else?"

"What else?" she asked.

"Give information, and take the £100," said her father.

"No, it would be mean and despicable to do that; and I should hate myself for ever after," replied Hannah.

"Then, shall we leave bad alone, and do nothing, and let Jim get the £100—for I fancy he knows already a great deal too much. But tell me, where is the child?"

"Down stairs, I think—at least she was there ten minutes ago."

"He didn't take her off with him, did he? I couldn't see him go from this window. He started from the back."

At this question, poor Hannah looked quite aghast. The possibility of little Mabel having been whipped up and carried off, without her stock of clothes and rattletraps, had never once occurred to her. "I'll go and look," she said.

A full quarter of an hour elapsed, and then the old man heard a buzz of neighbours' voices about the house. Their talk was of the child. Two of them asserted most confidently that they had seen the young Mr. Smith galloping up the hill in the gig, but that he was quite alone, and there was no Mabel with him.

Where, then, was she? What had become of her, for she could not be found high or low? Possibly she had toddled down upon the beach, and got lost amongst the rocks and pools, and the tide had come up and cut her off. What a horrible idea! But still it might be true. Where was she? What on earth had become of her? Some one thought, but could not be sure, that he had seen her in the garden, near the outhouse, when her father left.

"Do you think, Hannah," said the old man, "that he could have popped her into the locker of the gig? Was it large enough to hold her —she is a little creature?"

But poor Hannah could only wring her hands, and sob out, "No, she can't be there."

"I'm not so sure of that," replied her father, "and what is more, I am not sorry this has happened, for I can make it an excuse for writing to him. Quick, girl, and find a messenger to run after him to the town, while I write him a few lines."

They were as follow :—

"Mabel is missing. We cannot find her anywhere. I implore you to relieve our anxiety about her. My daughter is distracted, thinking that the tide may have surrounded her, perhaps. I beseech you also not to suppose me capable of betraying you. My only wish is that the happy state of things before our quarrel just now could be restored. I have known what I told you for two years, without betraying you, Why then need you doubt me now? Do not leave the Island until I have seen you, at any rate, once more. In the name of our old friendship, I ask you to forgive and forget, and to accord me this favour. I have also something of the utmost importance to reveal to you."

A man was found to carry the above note to Clifford's lodgings in the town. When he got there, he heard tidings of the child. In fact, he saw her. She had been brought there by Clifford in the gig, an hour or two before, but he had gone out again. The man, true to his instructions, would not leave the note in anyone's hands save his to whom it was addressed; and after waiting about, in vain, until nearly midnight, he walked back with it in his pocket, and returned it to the writer.

In the meantime, old Smith, without the knowledge of his daughter, wrote another note, ready to be posted at a moment's notice, and which ran thus:

" If Charles Marsden will multiply his promised

reward by ten, he shall receive at once all the information for which he has advertised. His reply to this intimation must be by another advertisement in the same newspaper, headed J. S. The sooner the better, as the culprit has already taken alarm."

The above was addressed as stated in the advertisement ; but in order that the Jersey postmark might not appear upon the envelope, it was enclosed in a wrapper addressed to an acquaintance in London, with a request that the enclosed note might be posted at the General Post Office, at St. Martin's-le-Grand.

" I would not do this," said the old man to himself, as he directed it, " except for fear of Jim, who is not to be trusted now."

CHAPTER 10.

—

A DRIVE.—HASTY RESOLVES.

How wonderful is the elasticity of some mens' temper—their buoyancy of spirit which nothing can keep down—their pluck which nothing can daunt—their insolent self-reliance which no amount of failure seems to quell. Clifford—for we must no longer call him Smith—was blessed with a disposition of this sort. Anyone would suppose that on his drive back to town that day, he would have exhibited a miserable picture of dejection and care, after his discovery that the old man at La Pulente knew so much more about him than was either pleasant or safe. But it was no such thing. After descending from the attic he looked about for Mabel in both of the lower rooms, but could find neither her nor Hannah there. Then he went round to the back

of the cottage, where he had put up the horse, and spied her playing in the garden, amongst the pinks and wallflowers, by herself. He said nothing, but put the horse into the gig, and then went and fetched her in his arms, popped her into the locker under the seat, and drove off. The little creature was not frightened, but delighted at the fun; and when he had gone a few hundred yards, he took her out and stood her between his knees. Then, away they went again. Like the son of Nimshi he drove along the country roads, and the child's spirits rose to a perfect ecstasy at the rate they went at, and the fun of leaving " old Jack " and Hannah so far behind, and having a ride with her dear Papa. Her merriment was contagious. The brow of her companion soon cleared up, and his laughter became as riotous as her own. Once, when they slackened their pace a bit to mount a hill, he tore up an old newspaper for her into little scraps, which he crumpled into pellets, and gave her by the handful to pelt the people with, by the road-side, when they dashed on again. It was true that Clifford loved young things. Some men do, and they show it all through life. The mere companionship of the little fairy of three years old, who was standing between his knees, routed the blue devils, and he was himself again. And yet he had already decided on leaving Jersey that night, in the BAGATELLE, for any port to which the fickle winds might waft her. He had decided also on another step, of a more interesting nature—as will appear in due time.

On they went, those two, in the gig, at the same rattling pace, even through the suburbs of the town, until on turning a sharp corner they almost knocked over a respectable old gentleman in black, who proved to be no other than a friend of the driver's—the Rev. Alfred Bell. So the horse was pulled up short, and the following dialogue ensued :—

"Mr. Smith! Is that you? Why, God bless me—you nearly drove over me, and extinguished the vital spark."

"Mr. Bell! My dear Sir! I beg you ten thousand pardons. But you're not hurt, or a man to be much frightened either. Besides, you're the very man I most wanted to see just now. Which way were you going? My way? Then do pray jump in, and let us have a chat. I've got a great deal to tell you."

"But not if you mean to drive like that, my good fellow. Remember, we are in the town now, and not at La Pulente. And who may this little darling be, with her merry eyes and rosy cheeks, Eh? I think I know her, bless her, though I've never seen her little face before. But you hav'n't surely brought her all this way without her hat?"

"Oh, that's nothing. I couldn't wait till she was dressed,—besides, she often runs about without her hat, don't you Maby? I'm going to leave her at my lodgings as we drive past, and then go on to the old harbour, to the yacht. Come with me, do, and dine on board,—for I shall be all alone to night, and as sulky as a bear with a sore head."

"I can't promise about dining," replied the old gentleman, "for I've left my youngest daughter all alone—her mamma and sisters having gone to an archery meeting somewhere out of town—and the invitation to which, I must tell you, came in very opportunely as a set off to their disappointment about the sail with you to-morrow. So I couldn't very well stay to dine with you, but I'll just go on board, with pleasure."

"Pray don't let that be a hindrance," said young Clifford, persuasively. "Let us call for Miss Kate, and take her too. The more the merrier, I always say — particularly when the addition to the party is a charming young lady of seventeen."

"No, no, — not to-day. It is very kind of you to offer, and say such pretty things—but—but — you know it wouldn't do to-day." And so saying, the worthy old gentleman in the black coat and white choker got into the gig, and they drove off together. Mabel was left with Clifford's housekeeper as they passed —who was much surprised, but at the same time delighted to have the charge of her— while in the quick transitions of a child's temper, the little one piped at first at seeing her Papa drive off, but was pacified the instant after; and in another five minutes the gig was brought up alongside the BAGATELLE.

It was about four o'clock, and high water at the time, so she was then afloat. They hailed Jim, and he put off for them in the dingey; and then a boy was found to take back the gig to the stable from which it had been hired. Thus, in a very few minutes, the owner of the yacht and his reverend friend were standing together on the deck.

It was evident, from half a glance at Jim, that his temper had undergone as marvellous a change for the better as his master's had, since their quarrel in the morning—for he was as civil and respectful as a man could be, and had been busy all day bending the sails, and getting ready for the little cruise and picnic which was to come off on the following morning. Something to do was, in fact, one part of the secret of this happy change of mood in Jim, coupled with the sincere wish to please a master whom he really liked immensely, and was sorry to have offended. Indeed, had anyone else dared to say to that kind master of Jim's half the saucy things that he had himself said that morning, he would have had his jacket off, and have tapped the fellow's claret,—for Jim was a true British tar at the bottom, every inch of him, and he swore by his young master, and thought him fit to be the first gen'l'man in the land—no matter what might be going on behind the scenes.

The visitor was shown into the cabin, and left there for an instant, while Jim and his master had a word or two privately on deck.

"Jim," said the owner, looking his man gravely in the face, "your impudence this morning has opened my eyes rather considerably, and what is more, it has got me into trouble with the old man at La Pulente. Now, just say yes, or no, at once,—are you and I to be friends any longer, or not?"

"Lor', Mr. Clifford, how can you be afeard of me? Why I'd rather——"

"Afraid, Jim? Stuff," replied his master. "I'm not afraid of anything—don't think that —only the old man, and you too, it appears, have got hold of a cock-and-bull story, which makes my stay here any longer out of the question—that's all—and I mean to make a bolt to-night. We had a tremendous row, and he threatened to have me arrested on some foolish suspicions of his, which would lead to nothing, only it would be very unpleasant for me, you understand."

"I thought as much," said Jim. "When I see'd you go off this morning in such a wax I thought you'd be going over there—and I knew what would come of that. So I just bent on the sails, and took off her legs, and filled the water cask, and it's only to put that old gen'l'man ashore again, and cast off from the buoy I moored her to, and up forestaysail, and round she goes, right before the wind, which is North-East, and fair for France. We'll be there in five hours if it don't come calm."

His master laughed outright. "Jim, my boy, you're a brick—give us your great dirty fist—I'll trust you, and that's enough. But I didn't mean to be off quite so sharp as that either. I've got a few little things to do ashore yet. In the night will be quite soon enough to start."

Jim looked thoughtful. "No, no, Cap'n, don't bide here. Off with you at once to some French port—and then I can come back in one of the little coasting smacks, and do anything you want done here. The old man is a crafty old customer, and if he means to nab you, it'll be done at once."

"I can't help that. I must take my chance. There are people I must see once more before I start. But I tell you what—suppose we cast off from here now, and take her outside into the small roads, and hold on to the mail-steamer's red buoy a bit, and keep a sharp look-out. The gentleman below is going to dine with me; and as soon as it gets dusk, if nothing happens, I shall run ashore with him, and be back again very soon. Then, if the wind keeps fair, and there's enough of it to stem the tide, we'll cast off for good."

" Ah, Cap'n," said his man, looking quizzically at him, " I sees how it is."

" But you know, I must fetch little Mabel on board. I'm not going to leave her behind, you blockhead."

" And who's going to look arter her, I wonder?" said the man, with a sly twinkle of his blue eye. " That old gen'l'man below—eh?"

" Pooh—hold your saucy tongue, Jim. Now just do what I tell you, and don't say a word. Cast off slyly—up jib and round with her—and then steer her out before the wind, while I go below and talk to him. I've got something to say to him. I don't want him to cut away. You understand?"

Jim tipped his master the wink, and very soon the little vessel was under weigh, and gliding slowly and noiselessly down the harbour, towards the open sea.

CHAPTER 11.

—

A PROJECT—A TÊTE-A-TÊTE.

CLIFFORD had no great difficulty in persuading his reverend friend to dine with him on board the BAGATELLE that afternoon, after they had moored her outside the harbour, in smooth water under the shadow of Elizabeth Castle—an island fortress about a mile from the shore. During their meal —which it must be confessed was a cold one, consisting of some of the viands which had been procured for the proposed picnic on the following day—and over the wine and dessert which followed, the host submitted to his guest a plan, to which the latter acceded, on the condition of its also meeting the approval of his family. It was this—that as circumstances had occurred to compel the owner of the yacht to leave Jersey suddenly for France with his little daughter, and therefore to put off the proposed sail and luncheon on the following day—the whole Bell family should take a trip across with him, in her, to St. Malo; starting as early as possible the following morning, and making the yacht their home when in France, for just so long as they might find it agreeable to themselves to do so.

The infinite coolness of such a proposition, coming from Clifford at such a time, and situated as he then was, will probably astonish and amuse the reader not a little, and exhibit a new phase of that young gentleman's character; but it may possibly scarcely astonish him more than the fact of the old clergyman's acceding to it, in the innocence of his heart, and the great personal liking he had for the author of the scheme. The only difficulty in the way of carrying out so agreeable a project seemed to be, the getting his wife and daughters up and packed, ready to start by six the next morning, on so short a notice. On the other hand, however, we are bound to state that previously to this invitation, Mr. Bell had actually contemplated taking his family for a fortnight's trip to the very port above-mentioned, during their summer holiday in Jersey,—so that the chance of going over in a yacht, with the fun and novelty of living on board of her instead of at a French hotel, added to the saving of expense, and the fineness of the weather just then, decided him on accepting his young friend's offer—conditionally, as aforesaid. But would his wife and daughters consent to the arrangement? That was just the hitch; and the only way to settle it was, to take Clifford home with him at once, and talk it over with them.

The sunset gun had just fired its one bang from Elizabeth Castle, as the two friends stepped into the dingey, and were rowed ashore by Jim. As the latter landed them at the steps at the harbour mouth, his master's last words aside to him were. "Stop here with the boat until I come back—which may not be for a couple of hours, or may be at any moment—and keep one eye on the yacht, and the other on the boats and people about here." Jim's reply need not be repeated, but it contained an allusion to his grandmother, and the art of sucking eggs.

The two friends then walked off briskly

together to the town. First they called at
Mrs. Brown's, and ascertained that " the little
innocent, bless her," had been duly put to bed,
invested in some borrowed night clothes; and
having thus assured themselves that Mabel had
been cared for, they proceeded to the clergyman's
own home, in the hired house on the pretty
terrace commanding the fine view over town
and sea. There they learnt that Miss Kate was
in the drawing-room alone — her Mamma and
sisters not having yet returned from the archery
meeting at Rozel.

The young lady was standing at the window
when they entered the room, enjoying in loneliness
and reverie the summer sunset over the distant
range of hills and placid sea; and it was as well
perhaps that the ruddy glow which suffused
her face as the visitor was announced was in
harmony with the crimson hues of nature
outside, and might be attributed to reflected
light rather than to any inward emotion of
her own. Certain it is, however, that as she
laid her little hand somewhat passively in his,
it received a pressure many shades warmer and
more expressive than it had ever received from
him before.

"So they've not come back yet," said her Papa. "How tiresome it is of them to stay out so late. Why, it must be near ten o'clock. Mr. Smith has kindly offered to take us all over with him in his yacht to France to-morrow; and as the wind is fair, and the weather so very fine, I have agreed to go, if your Mamma consents. But we must positively start at six, or even earlier if possible. Now, do you think, Katie, that we could all get ready, with your things packed up for a fortnight's trip, by that time to-morrow morning,—for it is very short notice, I'm afraid?"

"Oh yes, Papa, I am sure we could," said his daughter, vainly attempting to conceal her delight at the proposition. "Half an hour would be quite time enough for us to pack in— at least I think it would for me."

"But would the rest of you like to go, Kate? That's the question."

"Yes, Papa, I think they would. Ellen, I know would be enchanted,—and Sophy would like it too, I'm nearly sure."

"I am not so sure, however. But look—here they come."

As he said it, a large char-à-banc, drawn by

four horses, and containing about twenty people, drove up to the door, and Mrs. Bell, with her two elder daughters, were set down.

The old clergyman went at once to meet them in the hall—leaving Kate and Clifford alone together in the drawing room.

They were standing within the recess of the window at which Kate had been found when Clifford entered.

"Do you think your Mamma will let you go?" he asked, in his softest of accents.

"I am almost afraid not," she replied, looking down, and rather confused. "Mamma dislikes the sea so very much."

"But you and your sisters might go without her, surely?"

"That is almost too much to hope for."

"You would like it then?"

"Perhaps—I fancy so."

There was a pause for some minutes, and then Clifford spoke again.

"Kate," he said—and it was the first time he had ever addressed her by her christian name—"I am compelled to leave Jersey to-morrow morning, suddenly and for ever. If you don't go this trip with me, we may never meet again."

The young lady made no reply, but her little heart began to beat quicker than she had ever felt it beat before.

"Kate—dear Kate," he added, "my tongue must tell you now what my eyes, I am sure, have told you a thousand times before, that I love you dearly, and that if this is to be our last parting, life will have no more joy for me. Oh, say, then, that it is *not* to be—say that I may write to you—and may meet you again in England when you return home. Say so, dearest Kate, or this horrid parting will crush me quite."

He took her hand, and pressed it to his lips. She did not resist, but still looked down, and trembled.

"Kate," he added, "You love me—I know you do—Oh, happiness!" And as he said it he looked for a reply into her half-averted face. She was silent, and did not positively deny the charge. There was no more need for questioning, and Clifford stole his first embrace.

At that instant a noise was heard, and the door was seen closing gently, being pulled by some one from without. They both left the window, and went to the table in the middle of the room.

In the meantime Mr. Bell had met his wife

and two elder daughters in the hall, and had taken them into the dining room to hear his plan developed, and to endeavour to gain for it the approval of the higher powers. We will not repeat the various arguments, pro and con, which were advanced on either side. Let it suffice that not one of the three ladies consulted would agree to go. It was ruled, however, that Katie might go, if she liked, and if her Papa chose to take her, and saw no impropriety in doing so. The fact was, her Mamma and sisters had that day received two pressing invitations for the following week, which were more attractive to them than the proposed yachting trip.

"With respect to Katie going," said her Papa, "the poor child seems delighted at the idea of it — and she has been left alone all day in anticipation of a sail to-morrow — and she does not seem to have been included in either of your invitations for next week — and as I fully intend to go myself, it really seems a pity not to take her. Such a chance of a little yachting might never occur again in her whole life, and she will remember the fun and novelty of it ever after; besides which, she will be of use in looking after the child on the passage over, and will be a companion to me as well, and help me with the French. I hate going on a pleasure trip without some of you with me; and as for there being any objection to her going, on the score of propriety, I really don't see any — for I shall always be with her, and as soon as we get to France a *bonne* will be engaged to wait upon her, and remain with her on board. Well, then, it's settled that Katie and I, at any rate, will go."

The news was received by that young lady with just the proper expression of delight; and it was further arranged that a carriage was to be ordered to be at the door at five the next morning, to take her and her Papa and their luggage to the Pier Head, and to pick up little Mabel on the way. Clifford then took his leave, and spent an hour at his own lodgings; after which he strolled back to the terrace, by the light of the full moon, and for more time than he was probably aware of stood watching the shadow of a fairy figure, passing and repassing before one of the upper windows, as it was thrown upon the blind. At length, fearful perhaps of being observed by strangers, he turned away and walked quickly off in the direction of the Pier.

The dingey was still at the steps where he had left her, and Jim waiting by her side.

"There's been a man down here, Cap'n, enquiring for you," he said, in a low tone. (Be it known, that with Jim, his master's name was always "Cap'n" when there was any yachting going on, and "your honor" when the yacht was laid up); "and he had a letter which he wouldn't give to no one but yourself. I know the chap well. He's one of them vraickers out at La Pulente, and the letter was from our old man — a crafty old party that. Now, you mind Cap'n, what I say — if you stay lingering hereabouts all night till daylight comes, you'll be nabbed — and I'm afeard you don't mean to make a start, for you ain't brought down the child with you now. As for that chap — he got nothing out of me. I know'd nothing, in course — but Lor' how was I going to gammon him? Didn't he see the yacht outside, and me waiting here for you? Any lubber might have known you meant to give 'em the slip to-night. The chap had been up to your lodgings — and down here twice — but I knew where you was, well enough. Didn't you meet him nowhere, as you come along?"

"No, Jim, I've seen no man—but now I think of it, Mrs. Brown did say that a sort of sailor fellow had been up there, waiting about for me. But I can't start to-night—that's flat. I *must* stop till to-morrow. That old gentleman who dined on board is going across with us, and Mabel too — and they are to be at the Pier Head, in a carriage, about six — so we can't start before. Now, not another word, my good fellow—that's settled, and I must take my chance."

"Is the gen'l'man going to bring any young ladies with him, Cap'n?" asked Jim, in the most respectful tone he could assume—but the mock gravity of which was more comic by far than any sly chaff he might have ventured on, with a good-natured master.

"Well—yes, Jim—I think he is."

"How many on 'em are coming? I merely ask, because I must set about and get berths ready for 'em, as soon as we get aboard."

"Then arrange the ladies' cabin for one lady only, and little Maby," said his master; "and let us get aboard now as quick as we can.

But Jim, has any one been down with a lot of luggage of mine?"

Yes, Cap'n, it's all right—I stowed it away in the bow, and the small parcel is in the stern sheets."

"Well then, off with you."

With this hint Jim shoved off at once. As they were nearing the yacht his master said

"I wonder what that letter was about Jim, that the man had brought for me from old Smith."

"Don't you bother about that, Cap'n," was the reply. "Let him write to you in France, if he has got any last words to say. Don't you trust nothing to him. I know our old man well—and I could never work to wind'ard of him, or strike soundings on him either—ain't he a deep cove, my eyes! If he's got much to say to you, Cap'n, you jump on the other side of the gutter first — that's my advice. He can speak a chap fair enough—but he ain't got no honor in him like a real gen'l'man. Lor', don't he yaw, and wear, and tack about!"

"I think you're right," said his master, as he laid his hand upon the rail, and sprung on board the BAGATELLE.

CHAPTER 12.

—

A NIGHTLY VIGIL.

It was a heavenly night—not a cloud above, or a ripple beneath—the sea like a looking-glass—scarce a breath of wind stirring—and the full moon making it as light as day. The Bagatelle lay motionless upon the still water, as if asleep—with her mainsail and gaff-topsail set, like the folded wings of a great butterfly—her foresail down on deck, but ready to be hoisted at any instant—the fore-staysail the same—and the jib hauled out to the bowsprit-end, with the haul-yards hooked on to the head, and a stopper passed loosely round the foot of it, close by the stem. She was moored, it is true, to a great buoy, and lay with her head pointed to such little airs of wind from off the shore as would sometimes shake the peak of her gaff-topsail,—

but there was no tide running there, and the rope which held her to the ring hung loosely in a festoon, with no strain upon it but its own weight. There were no other craft near her, large or small, nor any boats about—the fishermen having all gone further out to sea.

It was midnight. Jim and his master—the only two on board—had already refreshed their inner men with coffee and sausage rolls, and were indulging in a glass of something hot, and a smoke on deck—the former with his meerschaum, the latter with his short clay pipe—the only visible motion in the scene being the smoke which they puffed forth, and that which rose in rivalry of it from the copper chimney of the cooking stove below.

"I say, Jim," said his master, good humouredly, after a long pause in their conversation, "tell me now, like an honest fellow, what you meant this morning, when you jeered me about the LURLINE and the Wolf Rock."

Jim took his pipe from his mouth, looked serious, and helped himself to another glass of grog.

"Come, Sir," said his master, "I'm waiting to hear."

" Well then—I 'll tell you, Cap'n—and truly too—I will, so help me Bob—I *will* tell you —there—that 's flat."

" You must. I shall be angry if you don't. The old man told me a deal more than I liked to hear—but he said nothing about the Wolf Rock. What do you know about that ? Come, tell me all, like an honest fellow, and let us have a fair start."

" So I means to do, Cap'n—but it aint much I 've picked up, after all—and I ought to have had my tongue cut out afore I blurted out what I did to you this morning. Well. then—there 's her old name, LURLINE, cut in the beam right over my own bunk,—and as for the Wolf Rock, why I saw something about a LURLINE yacht being wrecked upon it, in an old newspaper. There now—that 's all—it is, so help me——."

" Stop," said his master, " no lies, Jim. When did you see that in the paper ? How long ago was it ? "

" Lor' Cap'n—ain't you never seen it ? Why it was years and years ago—so long ago that I 've well nigh forgot all about it. I think it was a brig reported seeing her go down, after she struck, and all the crew in the gig capsized and lost. Her foremast was gone by the board, but there was a burgee of some yacht club flying at the mainmast head—and they made it out, and sent word to the Secretary—and he wrote to the paper. That's all I know about it, Cap'n—and it was a terrible long time back that I see'd it—but I think I've got the paper shoved away now somewhere down below, in the fore-peak, for I wrapped up my baccy in it for two years or more."

"Then go and get it Jim, as quick as you can, for I'd give the world to see it."

Jim did as he was told, and dived down through the scuttle into the forecastle with much alacrity; nor was he long in finding a paper containing an allusion to the Lurline and the Wolf Rock, but it was quite a recent one—in fact, the *Times* of the same date as that in which old Smith had seen the advertisement headed £100 Reward. This Jim no sooner found than he cut out the advertisement, folded it up neatly, and put it into his tobacco box, while he crammed the rest of the paper into the stove. He then waited a few minutes, in order to pretend he was looking for something, and mounted again to his master's side.

"I can't find it nowhere, Cap'n," he said. "It's clean gone—most likely burnt."

"The d——l," said his master, "that is unlucky. But try, Jim, and remember all you can about it. Was it an advertisement—or a notice—or what?"

"Shipping intelligence, Cap'n—just a short notice, for the comfort of surviving friends."

"And you've seen nothing more about it since?"

"Not a word, so help—I mean upon my soul, Cap'n, I hav'n't—but then it ain't often I reads a paper. What time has a poor chap like me got for that?"

"Did the old man see it?"

"No—that I'll swear he didn't—and that's why I kept it to myself."

"But tell me—what did you think about it, Jim?"

"Well now—I ain't going to tell you—that's flat—I ain't going to give you no more cheek about it—for Lor', I love you, my lad, as if you was my own son. If you like to put this and that together, perhaps you may find out easy enough what I think—and then you'll know. It's all one to me—I ain't going to leave you in your trouble, my poor lad—nor you ain't going to turn me off either. Now you knows what I mean. And I can tell you this here place ain't safe for you to lie in a single hour longer, now that you've quarrelled with the old man."

"But, Jim, I won't have you think badly of me—mark that. I've done nothing really wrong. If you think I have, off with you—for you and I shouldn't agree together for a single week."

"Lor,' now—what a fiery young chap you are. Why I swear there ain't a better young gen'l'man going. There—and as for doing wrong, let him as ain't never done it throw the first stone—as I heard our old man say once—and it's in the Bible too, I think."

"Well—I suppose it's no use arguing Jim, or trying to get anything more out of you. If you thought me very wicked, I dare say you wouldn't be here now, and sticking to me like a brick. So give me your fist, my man—and let us say good night—for I'm going to turn in, and you'd better do so too."

"No, no, Cap'n—here's my place—one of us must keep watch till daylight — and then

both of us together won't have eyes enough.
I 'll call you up when I want you—and I hope
at sunrise there 'll be a bit more wind—for
we sha' n't get two knots an hour out of her
if it keeps calm like this. It 's a regular paddy's
hurricane, blowing all ways at once."

Clifford shook the faithful fellow warmly by
the hand, and dived into the cabin below.
There he stretched himself upon his berth—
the same that he had occupied in years gone by—
when the blue Mediterranean was beneath her
keel—and in the ladies' cabin a young mother,
who had since been laid beneath the sod. For
an hour, or more, sleep came not to his pillow,
and he tossed about from side to side in the
restlessness of a mind which was ill at ease.
The past day had been a most eventful one
to him ; and he was then alone for the first
time with his own thoughts.

CHAPTER 13.

A START—CHASE OF THE BAGATELLE—LETTERS.

THE weather continued clear and calm throughout the night, and at length daylight dawned in the north east, chill and dewy, and the sun's red disc rose above the line of hills behind the town, in naked splendour, and with all heaven to himself. The wind had freshened up a little from off the land, but not much; and Jim, after a fashion of his own, prayed anxiously for more. As soon as it was broad daylight, he aroused his master from the deep sleep into which he had at length fallen; and then they both kept watch on deck, awaiting the arrival of the carriage at the Pier Head,—but nevertheless resolved to cast off instantly and make sail, should any treacherous looking craft pop out from the harbour mouth.

The hour of six arrived at last, and punctual to a minute the expected carriage hove in sight. Clifford insisted on fetching the party off himself, and no remonstrances of Jim's could keep him back. So far all had gone well, and he would listen to no hints of any possible danger from his rowing ashore. His greeting, however, to his friends, although cordial in the extreme, was hurried,—and he got them quickly into the dingey, and their luggage stowed, and then pushed off. Little Maby, who sat on Kate's knee, was delighted to see her Papa again, and to feel for the first time in her short life the motion of a boat; while the young lady who took such careful charge of her looked almost as radiant with glee, and her reverend father in high good humour too. The rower put forth all his strength to reach the yacht, and made both paddles and stretcher bend again to his vigorous strokes; and the dingey's bluff bow went surging through it, and left a long frothy wake behind. As now and then his eyes met those of the lovely girl who was seated opposite to him in the stern sheets, merry glances were exchanged between them,—while her kind father, by her side, was admiring in his own way the athletic form and handsome countenance of their young host. And thus the dingey dashed along and neared the yacht.

On their way the following short dialogue took place :—

"How many hands have you got on board this morning?" enquired Mr. Bell.

"Only Jim," was the reply. "One hand besides myself are quite enough for the run across, with a fair wind."

"Is it possible? Why, I thought you would have required four hands at least to work a yacht so large as that."

"Oh no—there are coasting smacks much larger than her, which ply between here and France, and only carry two men and a boy. The boy takes the helm while the men work the sails. The three are quite enough for a smack of fifty tons."

"But a schooner takes more hands than a smack, doesn't she?"

"No, fewer, because her sails are smaller."

"Then you'll be wanting one of us to steer sometimes, I suppose. Katie, you can steer our boat on the canal, and pretty straight too, can't you?"

"That's famous," said Clifford, smiling.

"Then, we'll make her work her passage over, while we look on and smoke. With beauty at the helm, a fair wind, a smooth sea, and a sunny sky, we ought indeed to feel ourselves in luck's way to-day."

By way of saying something in reply to this pretty compliment, the young lady remarked that the yacht, which they were then pretty near to, seemed to be turning round, and starting off without them, which she observed might rather interfere with their pleasant anticipations. At this intimation, the rower looked round, and saw, sure enough, that Jim had already cast off the rope from for'ard, and was hauling her stern towards the buoy, at the same time that both the jib and staysail had been run up, and were backing and making her head pay off. On looking aft again, to ascertain the cause of this sudden evolution on Jim's part, he perceived to his dismay that a boat which had just cleared the harbour mouth, with two rowers in it, was evidently giving them chase, while a man in the stern was standing up hailing them by waving his hat. At a sight which boded him no good, he at once redoubled his former efforts, and in a minute or two reached the yacht, which was then actually in motion, and put before the wind. Jim seemed too busy to offer them any help in scrambling up the side—for he was running hither and thither, pulling and hauling at ropes, belaying sheets, steering, &c., but saying not a word to anyone, and as cool apparently as if what he was doing had been all a matter of course; so Clifford himself made the dingey's painter fast to the main shroud, and helped his passengers on board, and handed them down below,—while the luggage was left in the boat for the present, and she was allowed to drop astern, in tow. Mr. Bell and Mabel were the first to dive through the cabin door,—but while their backs were turned, Clifford whispered softly to Kate to stay and take the tiller for a minute, while he and Jim set the foresail and foretopsail, as they wanted to lose no time, in order to save the tide.

The request was granted, with a smile,—and the young lady took the great tiller within her little palm, and obeyed, as well as she was able, the Captain's orders—if that is not too harsh a term. The foresail was then run quickly up; and the BAGATELLE, with her bow pointed towards the open sea, began to shoot a-head and make more way.

Unfortunately, however, the wind was light; and the boat in chase, which the two rowers were propelling with all their might, continued steadily to gain upon the yacht, until at length it was within pistol shot. A cloud then gathered upon Clifford's brow, which Kate, whose eyes were fixed upon him, did not fail to perceive; and on looking aft in the same direction as himself she at once divined the cause—the boat in chase! What could it possibly mean? and he showing signs, not of fear exactly, but of an anxiety which he could not conceal? Then she saw him go for'ard and consult with Jim for a few seconds; after which they both dived below, and returned quickly, Jim bearing in his arms a heavy pig of ballast, and his master a pistol, the stock of which stuck out as he crammed it into the side pocket of his coat. Then they both went aft and stood by the tuffrail, until the boat came fairly up, and hailed.

" BAGATELLE, a-hoy—Why don't you heave to for us—we 're well-nigh blown."

No answer.

" Is young Mr. Clifford a-board ? "

Still no answer.

A hand was then laid upon the rail.

"Stand from under," said Jim, sternly, "I'll heave this pig of iron a-board of you, and knock a hole in you, and sink you, if you come too close;—I will, by G——."

"Why, it's all right, Jim," said the man in the stern, reproachfully, who had been the first to hail. "We don't want nothing except just to pitch this here bundle a-board, and give the young gen'l'man a letter, and wait while he answers it—that's all. We've come from your old man up there yonder, at La Pulente."

"Oh, that's your game, is it?" said Jim. "Then chuck the bundle into the dingey, and chuck the letter a-board, and stand from under, and don't come too nigh, that's all. Catch a weazel asleep."

"What is it, my good fellow?" said Clifford, in a friendlier tone, "A letter for me—and a bundle? Well, never mind what my man says —make your boat fast and jump a-board, and you shall have a glass of grog apiece. There, carry that thing below again, Jim, we sha'n't want that—and haul the foresail to windward, and lay her to. Port, Miss Kate, please— hard-a-port—that's right—let her sails shake," and as he said it he jumped down by her side and hauled aft the main sheet. The yacht then luffed up into the wind, with her way stopped, her sails shivering and backing, and her bow pointing towards the shore.

So the boat was allowed to come alongside —the bundle was handed up—and the letter put into Clifford's hand.

As he ran his eye over its contents an angry flush suffused his face. He crushed the letter up into a mass, which he crammed into his pocket,—and he told the man who brought it to say that no answer would be given, for that he regarded both old Smith and his letters with supreme contempt.

The three men in the boat then tossed off each their promised potation of fire-water, and were cast off, to get back to shore again against wind and tide as best they could; and the yacht was put once more before the wind.

This scene was lost upon Mr. Bell, who had been below the whole time with Mabel; but he had heard the shaking of the sails, and the creaking of the main boom, and strange voices overhead.

" What have we been stopping for, Katie ? "

he enquired, as he came out into the fresh air, and took the tiller from his daughter's hand.

Clifford answered for her.

"My old friend Smith, at La Pulente, has sent a boat off to us, with a letter and a bundle containing Mabel's clothes. They will be very acceptable to the poor child, for we started in such a hurry that her outfit was rather of the scantiest."

This was said with a forced smile and a grim attempt at pleasantry, which may possibly have deceived the old gentleman to whom the remark was addressed,—but his daughter, who had witnessed the whole proceeding of the chase, could not but feel that some strange mystery involved a man, in whom a romantic interest on her part had been already confessed.

The yacht proceeded gaily on her way, and soon the cloud which the event at starting had cast across her owner's brow passed off, and to all appearance he recovered the gaiety and high spirits which for a moment had received a check. In a few minutes they had cleared the Violet bank, and then they jibed sail, and made for the eastern passage to

St. Malo, between the Minquiers rocks and the island of Chausey. The sails were trimmed afresh, the compass was uncovered, and Clifford took the helm himself—with his friends on either side of him, and with Mabel, who had quickly been rigged out in her own hat and cloak, racing and romping about in all a child's delight at the novelty of the scene. The vessel heeled over gently to the light breeze, and did her four knots, with scarcely a ripple at her bow, and glided noiselessly and smoothly across the glassy sea. Jim went down below, for'ard, to get the breakfast ready; and the smoke of the cooking stove was soon seen rising gaily from the copper funnel, while various savoury smells were wafted aft through the open cabin door. All went merry as a marriage bell. They had started at six, and would arrive perhaps at four in the afternoon, if the wind kept fair, and as it was,—the distance to be run being forty miles, or thereabouts.

Happily the wind kept steady and from the same point, and the day seemed made on purpose for them. And thus, noiselessly and smoothly they glided on, until the Maitre Isle was passed, and Chausey,—and the French coast came in sight, and Cezembre Island, and the City of St. Malo, and the Conchée Fort.

It was nearly two o'clock. Breakfast had been dismissed, and luncheon also—for yachting in fine weather, on a smooth sea, is hungry work—and once more the young lady passenger was at the helm, for she had owned to their gallant Captain that it was a greater pleasure to her to steer the yacht than her Papa's little skiff on the canal. So, with strict injunctions to keep Cezembre just seen above the weather bow—and with Jim to look out for'ard and see that all went right—Clifford left her side and went below. There, having shut himself up alone, he took from his pocket and spread out before him the crumpled letter from the old man at La Pulente, and read it over many times with deep attention. It ran thus:—

La Bic, 2 o'clock, a.m., June 21, 18—.

My dear young Friend,—If the man who is the bearer of this should have the good luck to catch you before you start, he will deliver into your custody a bundle also, containing Mabel's things—all except some rattletraps which it will be pleasing to us to keep in remembrance of her, and as a souvenir of the two happy years during which you were our

T

friend. But she is gone—and with her all our happiness has flown too—and Hannah and I are left to destitution, and as Job's wife said, to curse God and die.

That is the real fact. We are destitute, and what are we to do? I cannot now recover the broken threads of my former web, and resume my mode of life before you came to help us, and place us above want. I have therefore one of three courses left, viz., to die by my own hand—to die in a workhouse—or to raise money by betraying *you*. For this £100 are offered, and I have only to reply to an advertisement, and write a few words on paper, and *you* will be a ruined man. There will not then be a corner of this wide earth where the pursuers will not track you, and no country whose laws will not yield them the redress they seek. Your life will be like that of the flying-fish—a constant chase—to end in the fate of a galley slave, or worse. Murder, forgery, and robbery are the crimes of which you will be charged—and of the last two you will certainly be convicted, if caught.

You are therefore in my power; whilst I am in a state of destitution, from which betraying you would at once release me; for £100 represents four more years of life and comfort to my daughter and myself, in the humble way in which we live.

And now I will tell you what two courses are in their turn open to you. To despise my power, and brave the temptation which in my misery is put before me,—or to outbid the tempter by a higher offer still. Secure to me, then, a small annuity, sufficient for my humble wants, and you shall be safe from me.

Do you hesitate to grant me this favour? Then reflect on all that we have done for that dear child. We have saved her life,—for when Hannah first received her in her arms, her chest had ceased to heave, and but for Hannah's timely aid she would be lying by her mother's side in the churchyard; while since then we have carefully tended her and brought her up, and have taught her little tongue to prattle, and her feet to walk. Think of all this, and then ask yourself what *she* would do, if she were old enough, with her money, of which you constitute yourself trustee, if she were told that two of her three best and earliest friends were in deep distress, and that a little from her own abundance would rescue them from meanness, and yourself from a felon's fate.

I will say no more. I leave you to decide. It is not much I ask—and that not as a favour but as a duty which you owe to her and to us, as well as to yourself. Agree, and you shall be safe from me. Return to Jersey, and send her back to us, if you think fit; let all past unpleasantness between us be forgotten and forgiven, and let things go on as they did before.

Write me a line to say yes, or no, by the man who gives you this—and believe me still your friend.

J. S.

Having read the above letter many times, Clifford at length folded it and put it away.

He then opened his writing case, and answered it thus :—

I am sorry I sent you so hasty and angry a message back this morning, because I did not then perceive so clearly as I do now the line of conduct which I ought to pursue. My reply was such as I should always give to any man who insults and threatens me, or who meanly begs a favour of me; because it is my first impulse to reply to such a one with defiance, and with the toe of my boot. But your letter contained in the latter paragraphs a logic which I cannot resist. It is true that I have constituted myself a trustee for Mabel, and I must therefore act, not on my own feelings or impulses, but as she will approve when she arrives at an age to understand my conduct, both as a whole and in detail. To be brief, then, I agree to your request, because it would be only common gratitude in her, after all your kind and valuable services, to pension you for life. I shall post this as soon as we reach St. Malo,—and in the mean time I hope you will not have taken any rash or violent step, without at least writing to hear the result of my further consideration of your offer. I shall probably, under the circumstances, trust you so far as to return to Jersey in a fortnight, when my arrangement with you can be carried out. I must, however, decline to place the child again with you. My forgetfulness of unpleasant passages which have passed between us is impossible, but my forgiveness you have. That I still place some faith in your honour, and entertain some belief in your personal regard, let my future conduct testify. HENRY CLIFFORD.

The above was sealed and directed, ready for the post; and then, with a mind relieved from a load of care which had oppressed it more or less at intervals all day, the writer returned to his friends on deck.

He did so just as the BAGATELLE was abreast of the Jardin Beacon, and about to enter that dangerous passage amongst a labyrinth of rocks, known as the "Grande Porte," by which vessels commonly thread their way into St. Malo roads. But Jim knew the Channel well. Their last three miles of intricate navigation were passed in safety, and they dropped anchor off the town as the Cathedral bell tolled four.

CHAPTER 14.

ST. MALO—LA SANTÉ—PRESENTIMENTS.

THE BAGATELLE did not remain long at her anchor in St. Malo roads. A Government schooner, rather smaller than herself and similarly rigged, but with lug sails, presently sailed up alongside, hove to, and three *douaniers* jumped out of her into their boat astern, and pulled off to the yacht. After a few questions put with the utmost civility—for French *politesse* is a never-failing virtue through all ranks of society, so long as it meets with a suitable return—they made their boat fast and stepped on board. They then explained that no one was permitted to land from a strange vessel until their state of health had been inspected, and a free pass allowed. This announcement was received with much amusement by the yachting party; and Mademoiselle had the compliment paid her of being the first to undergo examination. But a glance at her bright eye and elastic form would have sufficed to convince even more sceptical judges than the sailors of the POTASS, that she, at any rate, was not likely to be the bearer of any infectious disorder to their port,—although, as one of them archly remarked, the *jolie jeune Anglaise* might still prove dangerous amongst his countrymen by introducing *maladies de cœur*. Clifford's turn came next, amidst a smile from all; and then little Mabel was trotted up and patted on the cheek. Lastly, the Protestant priest in his black garb and white choker was allowed to pass, with congratulations on his belonging to a sect which permitted him the privilege of possessing a family so very charming in all respects. At this the merriment of the party reached its climax, and Clifford intimated that he should in future take the hint, and call his lady passenger " Sister Kate." The matter of *la santé* having thus been quickly and pleasantly arranged, the men gave a look round the cabins, but quite as a matter of form,—and then requested to see the yacht's papers, and to be told her name. Happily there was no hitch there, and everything was strictly *en règle*. So the BAGATELLE was set down upon their book as belonging to Monsieur Jean Smith, member of the Royal Irish Yacht Club,—and the scrutiny was at an end.

It then became the owner's turn to put some questions to the men. First, he wished to know whether the yacht might be allowed to lie within the harbour instead of in the open roads, —and secondly, whether any of them could recommend a clean respectable *bonne* to attend upon the young lady, and take charge of the child during their stay in that port, which might extend to a fortnight or more. These queries received a prompt reply from all three men at once, accompanied with the full amount of French gesticulation. The yacht, they said, might be moored under shelter of the jetty, and left with her legs on, to take the ground,— and as for the *bonne*, it was a providential thing that the question had been put to them instead of to anyone else, because one of the *douaniers* had himself a daughter who would undertake the task, and whose natural powers, talents, bias of mind, and previous training were all such as to render her eminently qualified for the post of stewardess on board a yacht. The parent of this paragon moreover affirmed that if *Monsieur le Capitaine* should wish to take her to England with him, or even to the uttermost ends of the earth, she would be as *enchantée* to go as he, her Papa, would be to let her go.

So the end of it was, that with the help of the good *douaniers*, the BAGATELLE's anchor was hove up again at once, and she was moored in a snug berth beneath the harbour wall,—while a promise was exacted from the men that the *bonne* should be sent on board that night. The party then went ashore to take a stroll about the town—Clifford carrying little Mabel on his shoulder, and " Sister Kate " walking between him and her Papa.

St. Malo is one of the queerest little cities in France, or indeed in the world, and therefore the very port at which a visitor to the Continent for the first time should disembark. It is prettily situated at the extremity of a narrow tongue of land jutting out into the sea, near the mouth of the river Rance,—and is of course very small. High walls hem it in on all sides, and keep out air and light,—whilst the houses, which are mostly higher still, have steep roofs and tall chimney stacks, which break the sky line, and give the place picturesqueness from the sea. The streets are narrow and winding, with a gutter in the middle; and many of the houses have an antiquated *Prouty* look. But the chief characteristic of this little sea-girt city in a pill-box is its smell,—from which, however, you can readily escape by mounting the walls, on the top of which there is a promenade affording glorious views over the sea, the neighbouring coasts, and the islets which lie dotted around.

From the above description the reader will probably conclude, and truly, that our friends were better lodged on board their yacht than they would have been at the Hotel de France —at any rate in the sultry month of June.

At length the shades of evening were coming on apace—their first stroll was over—their first impressions had been formed—they had dined at a table d'Hote and had enjoyed the novelty of the scene no less than the good cheer— they had seen and engaged the *bonne*—the weary Mabel had been put to bed in the very berth which, as an infant, she had occupied

two years before—and again young Clifford
and his guests had started for another ramble
through the town. Backwards and forwards
they threaded the same labyrinth of narrow
streets, losing themselves perpetually but
coming always to one of the three outlets upon
the quays, and then returning in much
amusement within the maze. Slowly they
sauntered, stopping at this shop window and
at that, reading the names above the doors
— Simon, Charcutier — Ici on Rase—Veuve
Jacquart, Modiste—Nouveautés—Marchand Épi-
cier—Café Restaurant—Debit de Tabac—and
inspecting the strange articles which were hung
up to view outside, speculating, questioning,
commenting on all they saw in a scene so new
—at least to two of the party, who had never
been out of England before—and themselves
no less the subject of observation to the natives,
who smiled, and with a shrug of the shoulder
whispered to each other *"Anglais"*; and what
a pleasant stroll it was, on that first summer's
evening in France—and what a pity that Mamma,
and Sophy and Ellen had not come too—what
a loss to them—and how silly of them, was
it not?

All of a sudden Papa was missed! Kate and her companion had stopped, it seemed to them but an instant, to look into a shop window filled with crucifixes, pictures and images of the Virgin, tall wax candles, &c., and lo! in that brief space Papa had disappeared! How could it possibly have happened? The reader may smile, but truly no one was much to blame, for that little town is a perfect maze of streets, and a false turning leads you heaven knows where. Strangers should keep together in a place like that, particularly if they walk in threes. But where was poor Papa? What could have become of him? What would he do —for he could not speak a word of French? Had he been lost in Rome or Athens, Jerusalem or Thebes in the olden time, he might have got on well enough, — but at St. Malo in the nineteenth century he would be sadly at a loss. What was to be done? Surely he would not scold, for he must know that it was through no fault of theirs that he had slipped away. They thought he had been behind them all the time. So Clifford offered Kate his arm, that she might not lose him too, and they strolled on in search of her lost parent, little dreaming in their innocence that he had only popped for a moment or two inside the shop. Of course, the pair became quickly at a loss themselves in that labyrinth of streets, and the further they proceeded the more hopeless seemed their search, —until at length a winding staircase tempted them to mount upon the walls above. There they strolled again, and lingered, but Papa came not, — and at length they descended to the beach, where some bathing machines were seen, thinking it just possible that he might have eloped to take a dip,—but no, he was not there either. What were they to do?

"Suppose," said Clifford, "we extend our walk across the sands to yonder island, called the Grand Bey. I see some people walking there, and one of them, I do think, is your Papa. Let us go and see, shall we? It might be him."

Who could resist words of such persuasion, uttered in such a tone, on a lovely summer's eve—particularly in hopes of meeting with Papa? They went, of course.

The island in question can be reached on foot at dead low water, which it happened to be then; but Clifford had to help his fair companion over a rugged path amongst pools and boulders, which every tide disturbed. They crossed in safety, and he then let go her hand and offered her his arm again—regardless of the etiquette in France.

The persons they had seen were returning to the town, and the first they met was a gendarme. "*Monsieur* and *Madame* must not stay long," he said, "for the tide is coming up." The young lady smiled and turned away her face.

They mounted quickly some rude steps cut in the granite rock, and followed a winding footpath to the summit of the little isle,—but Papa could nowhere be seen from thence; then they descended on the opposite side to the ruins of an old fort, but he had not secreted himself there,—and lastly they followed the little path to the edge of a steep precipice, at which it stopped. The sea was roaring and surging a hundred feet beneath; and in front of them was the setting sun, with a bar of golden light upon the water, stretching to their feet.

"How grand!" said Kate. "There is surely nothing in Jersey to compare with this."

"If Sophy had said so," replied her companion, "I should have contradicted her flatly —should I not?"

" But my errors and delusions you indulge. I am to be a spoilt child always — humoured, laughed at, and never understood."

Clifford made no reply, but pressed her arm closer to his side, and continued looking at the setting sun.

" Let us sit down here," he said at last, "and rest a bit. You are tired. It has been a fatiguing day. You were up early this morning, and have walked about a good deal. See, the grass is nice and dry."

" No, not now," she answered. "The tide is rising, and we may be cut off—besides, it's getting late—Papa will wonder where we are —perhaps he will be angry—let us return at once and go on board—see, the dew is falling, and it begins to feel quite cold."

" But I ask it as a little favour," Clifford replied, "just one, to be granted me to-day. Let us sit here two minutes and watch the setting sun. This, you know, is the longest day. Let us stay and see it out together here, and make a note of it as an event in both our lives."

So they sat down together, side by side, upon a mound of turf, with the great and wide sea before them, and the sun sinking fast.　For some time neither of them spoke.

"If I were to live in yonder little town," said Kate, at length, "I should often come and sit here.　This would be my favourite walk."

"You like thinking," was the reply, "and that is why people say you are not so clever as your sisters, because they sing and play, and do their German and Italian best.　But I know you better.　I have dived deeper beneath the surface of your mind. You have more sentiment and imagination than they have—your vivacity is assumed—and your idleness a myth.　You will astonish us all some day by writing a tragedy, or a wild romance."

"And you—are not you a myth and a mystery?　People tell me so sometimes."

"And perhaps they add, *beware*.　Is it so?"

"Perhaps."

"And what do you say to that?　Do you tell them that you know me best?"

"Alas—I know but little of you."

"I understand you.　But you love me, Katie, do you not?　Happen what may, I may always count on that? I shall not be leaning on a broken reed, shall I? Suppose I were to become an outcast, destitute, friendless, with every man's hand against me—you would still believe in me, and love me—would you not?"

The poor girl made no reply. Perhaps he had put a question which she had already asked herself—for her heart beat quicker at his words.

As he ceased speaking, the sun's lower edge came down upon the sea. They watched him sink, in silence. The most solemn sight in nature passed before their eyes. As the last speck of sunlight vanished, Clifford laid his hand fondly upon Kate's, but felt it shiver at his touch.

" You are cold," he whispered tenderly.

" No,—but a sort of strange presentiment of trouble crept over me—a shiver, like a warning from the grave."

" Impossible! Who could have his grave in such a spot as this? But, naughty one, you did not answer my last question."

" Must I then?"

" Oh, do."

"And you won't be vexed? Well then—I have read, and I believe, that love is a deep and a holy feeling, based upon mutual confidences, and casting out all fear—that it is too enduring to be of quick or sudden growth—and that it is a sentiment running through one's whole life, and not a mere romance. But you forget how young I am—and how little I know of the great world. You have been very very kind —but—but—must I say it—I do not understand you quite. Oh, don't deceive me, or my heart would—I mean, I should be sorry to find you not exactly what I think."

"I comprehend you, Kate," he answered kindly, "but listen. Ever since my hopes were centered on your love I resolved to tell you my strange story, before things went too far. It is written, and you shall read it when you get back. Will you like to do so?"

"Ah yes—and now let us go—let us talk as we return—we have stayed away too long— Papa will wonder—forgive me if I said anything unkind just now—I did not mean it—do not think I doubt you. I never did, and never will."

"Bless you dear, dear Kate, for that," replied

her lover, as he helped her to rise from her seat upon the turf. "We will love each other always, whatever may befal me. But a strange awe creeps over me sometimes. Storm and darkness may be gathering round me—who can tell?"

"Oh, do not say so—you terrify me—what can I think of you when you talk like that?"

"Come then, let us go. I feel too some strange presentiment. Forgive my folly, but I have lived too much alone of late. Strange fancies sometimes haunt me. How chilly it feels here. Come, my Katie, let us go."

Some years after the above scene occurred, the renowned Chateaubriand was buried beneath the very spot on which the pair had sat that night. His tomb may now be seen there, surmounted by a granite cross, and protected by iron rails. It is one of the lions of the place. He was a native of St. Malo, and in his will he expressed a wish to be buried on that rock.

On their way back, Clifford said

"Three times in my life has the longest day been an eventful one to me. It was on the longest day last year that I first met you,

Kate—do you remember—at a picnic, when you came over to Jersey alone, on a visit to your Aunt? Our tablecloth was spread on a wild spot such as we have left. Two years ago, on the longest day, the yacht was cast ashore at La Pulente, and I came to know the Smiths. To-day has been an eventful one, too. In the morning you saw me fling defiance and contempt at a man who may have great power to injure me,—but in the afternoon I repented, and posted a submissive letter to him. And now, in the evening, you and I are walking alone together for the first time, and we have seen the sun set in the sea."

"But I cannot fancy you submissive," she replied.

"Do you think I have a cold proud heart? No, I hav'n't. But I am passionate, and much too rash for safety. Caution is a virtue that I have yet to learn. May we never need it, Katie."

They walked on quickly for some time, and not a word was said. At last Clifford broke the silence, in a gayer mood.

"Do you know who you remind me of?" he asked.

"No—who?"

"You are like a little bust from the antique, which I saw in a shop window an hour ago, as we passed. I will buy it for you to-morrow. It is a copy of a large one in the Vatican. I have got a cast from that at home. It is one of the nine Muses. Which of them, now, do you think you resemble? Can you guess?"

"Papa sometimes calls me the laughter-loving Aphrodite—but she was not a Muse, I think."

"He is mistaken. He does not know you half so well as I do. The Muse whom you resemble most is her of Tragedy."

"Melpomene? Oh, surely not. She is a monstrous Amazon—and I am not much above the middle height."

"And light and graceful as a deer. But you are Melpomene for all that. I mean her of the Vatican. You are thinking of the Muse in the British Museum."

"Do you mean that little bust we saw, with a mass of foliage round the head? Oh, surely I am not like her?"

"But your Papa admits the likeness too. When he first saw it in my rooms he said, why that's like Kate. I brought that cast from Rome, and it has always been my beau ideal of a lovely face. Shall we go there Katie, in the yacht, one day, and tow her up the yellow Tiber, and live on board?"

"Why, where on earth have you two been?" said the lost Papa, suddenly pouncing on them as they emerged from under a gateway upon the quay. "I lost you all of a sudden two hours ago. I just went into a shop for an instant where they wrote up "English spoken here," and when I came out, behold you were nowhere to be seen. I have been hunting for you ever since."

"Then it will be funny to compare our logs," said Clifford, "for we have been all that time in search of you. But how are we to get on board now, for I see she's high and dry?"

"And knee deep in mud all round. You are a nice Captain not to have thought of that."

"But how are we to manage it? It must be a case of pig-a-back, I think."

"No—I have engaged a cart to take us alongside."

"A bright idea—I should never have thought of that."

In a cart then they were put on board.

The reverend Papa said little, and did not scold,

whatever may have been his thoughts; and as they were all weary with their first day's pleasuring, they soon retired to their respective berths.

CHAPTER 15.

REPORTS—SCANDAL—FRIENDSHIP—LOVE.

CLIFFORD made but one nap of it that night, and when he awoke, the sun, which he had seen set the evening before, was shining gaily through the cabin skylight. He looked for his companion on the opposite berth, but Mr. Bell was up, dressed, and off—and yet by his watch it was only half-past five. Then he listened, but all was quiet in the forecastle, and Jim must have taken himself off too. On looking aft towards the ladies' cabin, he perceived the door ajar, and presently heard Mabel's loud and merry laugh, and the *bonne's* reproof. At last he understood that Kate and her Papa had already started for a walk, and taken Jim with them. What a shame not to have called him. He dressed quickly and went on deck. The dingey was at the slip, left in charge of a soldier on duty. He had therefore no means of getting ashore. By - and - bye, however, a passage boat full of market people from the opposite village of Dinard hove in sight, and as they lowered their great lug sails and ran in, he hailed, and they passed near enough for him to spring on board, and land with them. Then his instincts took him to the Market, and there sure enough were his Kate and her Papa, and Jim alongside, with a large basket already nearly filled with good things of all sorts, including fish and strawberries for breakfast. The meeting was a joyous one on all sides, but not without reproaches and expostulations from Clifford— to which his reverend friend replied

"Nonsense, my good fellow. You keep to your province and navigate the ship, and let me be caterer—that is my department, which I flatter myself I understand a deal better than you do. Jim, suppose you take the basket aboard, and come back and get the hot rolls. You remember the shop, don't you?"

"Ay, ay, your honor. This ain't the first time I've been to this here town."

"But Jim, how about the tide? It's going down, isn't it? Let us understand that, for it's awkward when she's high and dry."

"She'll float to-day from three till half-past eight, and an hour later to morrow," replied Clifford.

"Then we must have breakfast ready at the latest by half-past seven, or we sha'n't be able to land in the boat afterwards, eh, Jim?"

"All right, your honor, I'll have it ready. You leave that to me. The tide never don't cheat me."

"Well, then, we've got a good hour for a stroll. Which way shall we go? What is that town opposite? Is that too far?"

"St. Servan," replied Clifford. "I was thinking it would be fun to go there after breakfast in a one-horse trap. There's plenty to see in this neighbourhood—Dinard, Cancalle, the river Rance, Dinan, and perhaps we might manage a day or two to go and see Mont St. Michel."

"Well, anything you like. This change is really charming to me—quite a new sensation—but where shall we go now, that's the question. We've seen the town. Where did you two go last night? Kate, my child, you don't speak a word this morning—what's the matter?"

"Oh, Papa—how can you say so? I've been talking the whole time."

"Last night," said Clifford, with desperate truthfulness, "we strolled to a neighbouring island, but the tide is round it now—and we took a turn on the walls—and down to a bit of beach where the bathing machines are kept."

"And Papa has been there this morning," said Kate, "and I have had a dip."

"In tunic and trousers," said her father, laughing, "along with a dozen other girls,—and there was a priest amongst them in the water, with a long black robe, and a three-cornered hat on. Who would believe that, out of France?"

"And I was fast asleep all the while," said Clifford. "What a shame!"

Come, then, let us mount the walls and get an appetite for breakfast, "said Mr. Bell gaily, and offering Kate his arm.

After making the circuit of the town they came at length opposite to where the yacht was lying, and there they rested for a time, leaning on the parapet, watching the grey smoke rising from the copper funnel, with its queer shaped cowl.

"I am no judge of yachts," said the parson, addressing her owner, "but she looks to me a very pretty one.   Now tell me candidly, do you consider her a perfect model, and all that sort of thing ?   Are we to brag about our trip in her, when we get back to England—or not ?"

"Well, according to some tastes she would be thought perfection—but *I* think her model all wrong, from stem to stern.   Her bottom is horribly wedge-shaped, and she draws a great deal too much water — besides being too full for'ard, and too lean aft."

"You must write all that down for me, or I fear I shall forget it before the day's over.   But if you don't admire her, why not sell her and build another, more to your own taste ?"

This was touching on delicate ground, and Clifford replied, with some slight embarrasment

"I have associations with her.   She was left to me by my Uncle, about two years ago—and with all her faults I mean to keep her—at least until Mabel comes of age."

"That is, for eighteen years !   How we talk of years to come, at your age !   Happy youth !

But, ah, my friend, many an odd thing may happen before Mabel comes of age."

"Look, Papa," said Kate, anxious for her lover's sake to change the conversation. "Jim is coming ashore again in the little boat."

But her Papa took no heed of her remark.

"Did you ever hear of a yacht named the LURLINE?" he enquired of his friend.

This was dreadful; but Clifford did not lose his presence of mind. Happily the eyes of his companions were turned away from him at the moment, and he was able to answer boldly

"Yes. That was once the name of the BAGATELLE. But why do you ask me?"

"Because my wife and daughters heard some strange rumours about you in connexion with a yacht of that name, the day before we left Jersey."

For some moments there was a pause, and then Clifford answered in a cold and altered tone

"You surprise me, Sir,—or rather you torture me. I conjure you to tell me plainly what rumours they have heard."

"That is surely needless," replied Mr. Bell, in the kindest tone. "Am I not here now as your guest, and is not my child, whom I dearly love, your guest also? You must feel that if we had not both implicit faith in you we should not be here. Why then ask me to repeat unpleasant rumours which it is evident I disregard? I will even say more than that. So far from these surmises and reports about you having had any effect in deterring me from joining you on this trip, they helped to decide me on doing so. I have not known you many months,—but quite long enough to form a high opinion of you, and to entertain a regard for you. I therefore felt it a sort of duty I owed you to show, by my example, how little importance I attach to ill-natured remarks. If I should prove to be mistaken in you, then all I can say is that half a century of experience of human nature will be worth nothing, and at sixty I must begin again to learn; and yet it is my profession to read and try to understand the human heart."

"You are very kind, dear Sir—very—to put faith in me—and I shall never forget it. But may I beg of you most earnestly to tell me what those rumours were?"

"Nothing, I assure you, but what went in at one ear and out at the other. We may hear sometimes unpleasant things about a friend, because we cannot help it ; but our duty is, at any rate, never to repeat them."

"But I will find out, when I return, who my accusers are, and what they mean—the filthy jackals," said Clifford, in deep anger.

"No ! There you would be very wrong. The proper way to treat scandal is to take no notice of it, and live it down. It has always this good effect, although an evil in itself—it proves to you who are your true friends, and who are not. Those who are not you can continue to treat civilly, but nothing more,—while those who are come in for a larger share of your esteem by just so much as the others have lost."

"But still I should like to know what it is they say about me—and what foundation they have for it."

"Don't trouble yourself about the matter. You can easily imagine it all. You have only to seek in such facts as you know to be true, for the foundation of reports, and then imagine how they can be coloured and perverted—not always out of sheer malice, but from a low order of mind which takes delight in disparaging and finding fault. It is astonishing how much evil-speaking and slandering there is in the world,

even amongst persons who ought to know better.
Meanness is a very common vice, and generosity
a rare virtue. Let us all try to practise it much
more than we do, and make it enter more largely
into every thought and action."

"But I do not ask for generosity," replied
Clifford. " I demand justice as a right,—and
justice I would have from an assailant."

"You are angry and excited," said Mr. Bell,
" and I regret that I made that unlucky remark.
It was very thoughtless of me, I own,—but if I
had attached the slightest importance to what I
heard I should not have done so."

" I am sorry too," replied the other, " that I
should have shown such a burst of temper. But
since we have broached this subject, let me ask
you how a true friend should really act in the
event of hearing slanderous reports which have
a strong show of probability to support them."

" In that case, he would simply obey his
generous and affectionate instincts," was the
clergyman's reply. " If one's dog were in
trouble one would not desert him — far less
one's friend. Friendship is not based on the
supposition of perfection, for no man is perfect.
On the contrary, any man may fall, or why do

we pray 'lead us not into temptation'?   If then our friend should fall we must not leave him in the mire, but strive to pull him out, and set him on his legs again."

"But suppose that in his fall he should have broken both his legs, and be unable to stand again; or suppose that the mire should stick so closely to him that no one could touch him without being himself defiled; what then?" asked Clifford.

Mr. Bell answered

"You put an extreme case, but my reply is still the same.   A man must never desert his friend.   He must be found by his side to protect him from insult — he must be found by his side in the cell of the criminal — and he must be amongst the last to leave him if he should be led forth to the convict-ship, the gallows, or the guillotine."

"And these are the principles on which you would yourself act — and which you instil into your children?"

"I hope so."

"But if you should find yourself deceived in your friend.   If you should discover that he had never been worthy of your regard,—that, in fact, he had been an impostor from the first ? ''

"Then I should have to suffer from an error of judgment ; but still, once having entertained friendship for him would have given him a place in my heart.''

"Your sentiments are noble, my dear Sir,—may they never be too severely tried in real life. But we must go now. I see Jim waiting for us at the slip.''

As Clifford said this, he rose from his stooping posture on the parapet, and on turning to leave perceived Kate's eyes bent upon him with an expression of deep and tender interest. The momentary glance which they exchanged acted on him like a talisman. In an instant, doubt, anxiety, anger vanished from his mind, and hope stepped in again. With the singular buoyancy of his nature he seemed to forget at once, or to defy the hints which had been dropped of the danger in which he stood, and he lived only in the present. They all returned to the boat in better spirits even than before that strange dialogue took place.

CHAPTER 16.

—

LEHON ABBEY—DINAN—CHATELIER.

WE are not writing the diary of that yachting
trip, or it would be a pleasing task to recount
in order the adventures of each day of a happy
fortnight, as it glided, as happiness is said to
do, away. But a record of these events was
kept, nevertheless, by one of the party ; and
the reader's instincts will tell him which of
them it was. These notes, or jottings of each
day's adventures, were made by Kate, at such
odd times as opportunity offered, in lead pencil,
in a little book with a lock and key which
Clifford bought for her in St. Malo ; and not
unfrequently with him at her elbow as she
wrote. Sometimes even he would write a few
lines in it himself—and generally in a comic
vein—so that there were pages in it where

his own writing might be seen mixed funnily with hers. After the lapse of years, that little book, with its half-effaced contents, came back into his own possession, and then he observed in many places the traces of a tear. Life has its alloy of evil, more or less; and a diary of the past must always come to be, sooner or later, a mournful thing to read.

We shall not dwell long on that happy fortnight in the BAGATELLE. The reader must imagine much of what occurred, in the midst of thorough harmony and perfect understanding on all sides. Not one of the party ever forgot those happy hours—not even the little prattling toddling child, for some incidents of that yachting trip were amongst the earliest impressions engraved upon her mind. By turns they visited all the places which Clifford had enumerated on the first day—Mont St. Michel being that which delighted them the most; while these excursions were rendered infinitely amusing by the odd sorts of novel vehicles in which the party were conveyed, and the odd shifts to which they were sometimes put. And all this followed by their funny home on board the yacht,—for the feeling of home, when they returned to it after a temporary absence, cast a romance over their wanderings which no ordinary style of travelling permits.

On the last of these excursions, while Clifford sat with his sketch book on his knee before the ruins of a fine old abbey amongst the trees, his reverend friend joined him, and for some time seemed greatly interested in the progress of his work. They were alone, for Kate and Mabel were having a merry romp together in a meadow, a few yards off.

" So fond as you are of Art," said Clifford, " I am surprised you never took up the brush yourself."

The old Clergyman replied

" I have had other brushes to paint with, my young friend, than camel hair, and other subjects for my study than ruins and trees. You see me now indulging in a holiday which has become a necessary change after many uninterrupted years of toil. At home, in my little rectory, I am quite another man—as I trust you will find out for yourself some day."

" It is very kind of you to say so," replied Clifford, " for I cannot but feel that there is more couched in such an invitation than the mere words convey. May I live to convince you that I appreciate your great kindness, and am not altogether unworthy of it."

" Do you know that I rather pride myself on being a judge of character ? "

" I can believe it, for during the last fortnight I have often felt that your eyes were upon me, taking notes."

" But you did not quail beneath them—and you guessed that I had no wish to interfere with your designs—and that I was satisfied of your honourable intentions, eh ? "

" I felt that you tacitly encouraged them— and I was infinitely grateful for your kindness."

" Then, before our return home together, we have a little confidence to exchange on a delicate subject, have we not ? "

" By all means. Now, if you please. I am willing," said Clifford.

" Good,—then let us have our gossip now. We have time to spare for it, and both time and place are fit. Let me tell you then my own tale first. It was about two months ago that I first discovered that an attachment was growing up between yourself and my dear Kate, and then I began to observe and to analyse your character with much interest. But my most anxious study of it only dates from the evening before we started for this trip. You remember when I left you both together in the drawing-room for a few minutes, while I went below to consult with my wife and my other daughters about their accepting your invitation to go to France with you in the yacht? Well,— on my return to tell you the arrangement we had made, the door of the room happening to be ajar, I entered without disturbing your tête-a-tête. You were both standing within the recess of one of the windows, with your backs towards me, and you did not hear me approach you over the soft carpet, until I came near enough to overhear, but without any design or suspicion on my part, *your* ardent protestations of affection as you held her hand in yours. At such a moment I felt, of course, that it would have been a meanness in me to act the eaves-dropper, and I immediately left the room without either of you imagining that I had witnessed what I did. I returned shortly after, and found you both expecting me. A glance at Kate's happy face was enough. I knew how your proposal had been received; and you remember the message I brought up, as regarded the trip.   But I had learnt your secret, and it gave me food for anxious thought that night.   Would it be right and prudent, I asked myself a hundred times, to join you, after such a scene, and with her ?   But all I knew of you was greatly in your favour, so far as my own observation went, and I resolved therefore to trust you, but at the same time keep a careful watch,— for I have already intimated that my wife told me that evening of some rumours which she had heard about you during the day.   These, however, were very vague, and I reckoned them at just so much as ill-natured reports are commonly worth which suggest conduct at total variance with a man's general habits of life. When I hinted at these, on the second morning of our trip, your manner satisfied me of your integrity, but it led me to believe that a mystery of some sort nevertheless involved your circumstances.   If this should be so, I trust you will explain.   But understand me—I merely ask you for this confidence because it is essential to happiness between near and dear friends that there should be no concealment in these matters. If you were without a penny, and I had confidence in you and liked you, I should simply say, wait until you can support her, and then your union shall have my full consent. I must say, however, that the suddenness of your proposal that evening startled me, and took me greatly by surprise, for I had then no idea either that your feelings or hers had gone to such a length."

"But you must remember, dear Sir," replied Clifford, "that I have known Kate for a longer time than you suppose. I met her a year ago when she came over on a visit to her Aunt,—and although it is true that I had never been to her own home before the evening you speak of, yet I had often met her on other occasions, at parties, pic-nics, and so forth. It was, in fact, a sudden change in my circumstances and prospects, revealed to me only that day, which convinced me how much I loved her, and how deeply I should have felt a separation from her, unless some mutual pledge had been exchanged."

"But the nature of that sudden change in your circumstances and prospects you will confide to me, will you not?" said Mr. Bell.

"I will indeed, most frankly," replied Clifford. "You shall know all. But mine is a long and a painful story, too harrowing to tell you by word of mouth. I have written it all out expressly for you to read some day, and the manuscript is now on board the yacht."

"Has Kate seen it?"

"No."

"Then the sooner I read it the better. Suppose you give it to me to-night."

"No, not to night," said Clifford. "Grant me one favour. This happy little trip—let that pass over first. Then, read it when you get back to Jersey. That will be quite time enough. Nothing presses. Things may go on for years as they have done; in fact until Mabel comes of "age."

"Well then, we will say no more about it now; but if I have expressed a shade of solicitude it has been on my dear child's account—for there are moments when even in her presence your thoughts seem far away."

"It is true," said Clifford, "a slight cause of anxiety has arisen lately to disturb my peace. In fact, I hardly knew, when we left Jersey, whether I should return with you myself, or send Jim with a couple more hands to take you back again without me. A letter, however, which was brought to me that morning by the boat decided me to return with you."

"How strange!" said Mr. Bell. "But that little trouble has now passed off?"

"Trouble!" replied Clifford. "I don't know the word. I am in heaven—in a paradise of hopes and bliss. My happiness seems almost too great to last. I can scarcely realise it. The very cloud which passed over me has been a blessing, for its shadow revealed to us both how sincerely we were attached."

After a pause of some minutes in their conversation, the old clergyman said, with deep feeling in his tone,

"My poor Kate! Do you know, Sir, you are stealing away from me my favourite child? Ellen has a charming loveable disposition too, but in Kate there is more force of character, and more mind. In her's you will find a rich field to cultivate, and you will be repaid. She may be less accomplished than the others, but what she knows is sound, and her taste is more refined. She is a lady, in the highest sense, and with all a woman's true and generous instincts. I can see already that she loves you with devotion—and I have not opposed her choice, for I fully believe that she has chosen well. Had I not thought so we should not have been your guests. May you be happy in each other's love—and may I live to see it. My children are now my last stake in life, and my chief care. I do not covet wealth for them, or station, but simply an honest happy home, where love presides and where intellect lends a grace. There—I will leave you now— for my old heart is full."

With these words, the kind old man got up and strolled away.

It was the last day of their holiday ashore when the above conversation took place. The yacht, notwithstanding her great draught of water, had been towed up the river Rance, by a passenger steamer, as far as the pretty town of Dinan, about sixteen miles above its mouth, and four above the first lock,—and the party had that day proceeded three miles higher up still, in the dingey, to Lehon Abbey, and had there picnic'd and spent the afternoon. Thus it was their last day amidst the placid wooded scenery of the interior, and on the morrow the storm-beaten coast and the unquiet sea were to welcome them back again. That very evening, indeed, it had been arranged that the yacht was to be towed down by a horse to the first lock, at Châtelier,—and at daybreak the next morning they were to take to their long oars, and drop down the river with the ebb tide, and then, without stopping at St. Malo, stand on straight for Jersey, should the wind and weather permit.

It was already time to start for Dinan in the dingey, and Clifford was tying up his sketch book, when Kate joined him.

" Are you ashamed of your performance, that you won't let me see it ? " she asked, with a smile.

" The fact is," replied her lover, " I have not done much this afternoon, for at first I was watching you and Mabel at play, and then your Papa came and sat by me, and we had a long talk about *something*, and he invited me to the Rectory, and I accepted. Is not that good news ? "

The young lady blushed, but it was with joy. Her lover drew her fondly towards him, and added

" But you have now, Kate, a rival in my regard. It is your dear Papa. Look at the kind creature—he is leaving us together, that I may tell you about all this happiness. He has given his full consent. In another month, perhaps, I may call you mine—only fancy—in another month."

"But I came to see your painting; show it me, please," she said, evasively.

So he opened his sketch book, and there she beheld the old abbey and the majestic trees, roughly rendered by a few broad touches, but true to nature as true could be. It was the best sketch he took on that trip, and the last sheet upon the block. The rest of the drawings were in the pocket of the book. They had all been taken during that happy fortnight. As he handed the last sketch to her to look at, he said

" Keep this book, for my sake, and never part with it. Every sketch in it is full of associations, and eloquent of the past fortnight's happiness. Look at them sometimes, Katie, when you are alone, and think of this happy trip when they were taken."

" How pretty the one is which you have done this afternoon," she answered. " I like that the best of all. How truthfully, and yet how rapidly you paint. Your sketches always suggest beauties in the view which I did not perceive before—and yet all done with a few touches of the brush. What a marvellous art it is. How ever did you learn it?"

"Would you like to do it too? I know you could, and I will teach you. You will soon beat me. I have too bold a brush, and not enough detail. I could never get beyond a sketch,—but with you, Katie, sitting by my side, I should be able to paint on the same spot for ever, and never finish half enough. Oh, happiness! What a trip we've had—and to end in all this joy—and more to follow—without end! Do you remember what I told you that first night, just when we met Papa?—the yellow Tiber, and my dear old Rome? Shall we go there in the yacht this autumn, and take him, and Ellen too?"

"And leave poor Sophy and Mamma behind?"

"Poor Sophy," he replied. "Yes, I like her too."

"And not Mamma?"

"Oh, yes—if only for your sweet sake."

They strolled together to the dingey, which had been tied up under a summer house in the Abbey grounds, and then Clifford rowed them back, while Kate steered, and her Papa and Mabel sat on either side. How lovely the little river looked that night, winding so tranquilly between lichen-covered granite rocks and wooded slopes, reflected in it like a glass. What a heavenly summer's eve it was. What a rich golden light. What a scene to be remembered for the rest of life !

At length the town was reached. Their last row in the little boat was over. Swiftly they shot beneath the lofty viaduct—then but half completed, and now one of the finest engineering works in France—and then through an arch of the picturesque old bridge. The yacht was at the Pier close by, and a horse already waiting to tow them to the lock. They stepped on board, and at once cast off. Again Kate steered ; and again, in the glow of a summer sunset, her lover was seated by her side.

CHAPTER 17.

—

A BETRAYAL—A NEW ACTOR IN THE SCENE.

LEAVING our friends to their repose in the cabins of the BAGATELLE, on that, the last night of their trip to France—as she lay moored in a sort of basin of deep water just above the lock at Châtelier—we will step across to Jersey and see what had been going on there during their fortnight's absence from the island.

One of the men who had rowed after the BAGATELLE in the boat which gave chase to her on the morning of her start for France, conveyed Clifford's defiant message to old Smith. The old man sat up in bed, had it thrice repeated to him, put many questions respecting the chase of the yacht, her probable destination, the name of the young lady who had been seen on board, and the conduct of Clifford from first to last. He then put into the man's hand a letter which he requested him to post on his return to the town, and dismissed him with his fee.

That letter was a reply to the advertisement in the *Times*, in which £100 reward had been offered for information respecting the fate of the LURLINE, &c.   It ran thus :—

If Charles Marsden will communicate with John Smith, of La Pulente, in the Island of Jersey, the latter will furnish him, for the reward stated in his advertisement, with full particulars of all that he requires to know.

The above letter was addressed, as directed in the advertisement, to Charles Marsden, Albion Coffee House, Southampton; and the boatman posted it that same day.

About a week after, a visitor was announced at La Bie.   It was Charles Marsden himself.

He was a man of middle age, rather tall, of slight figure, and in appearance what is called "shabby genteel."   His hair was light coloured and long, and he wore a moustache and beard trimmed in the French style.   His gait was feeble, and like that of a man many years older; and his .face, which was of a sickly cadaverous hue, bore testimony to a constitution which had been broken by early habits of dissipation. Its expression, moreover, was characterized by a concentration of purpose, and that not a benevolent one. On the whole, the appearance of the man was disagreeable, and not such as to inspire the confidence of a stranger.

His arrival was announced to old Smith by Hannah, who was requested to show him up at once into the attic. At that time Clifford's apologetic letter to Smith, written on board the BAGATELLE on the first day of the trip, and posted the same evening at St. Malo, had not been received. It had been lying two days at a post-office a couple of miles from La Pulente, and had not been sent for, or forwarded.

The visitor walked up to old Smith's bedside, and announced himself as Charles Marsden, from Southampton,—adding, " and you, I suppose, are the John Smith who answered my advertisement."

" I am," replied the old man.

" Then let us proceed to business at once," said the other. " Have the goodness to listen attentively to the following story :—About two years ago, I left my wife Zoe, together with her infant daughter Mabel, and a young man named Henry Clifford, on board a yacht named the LURLINE, which was then in imminent danger of destruction in a gale, off the Cornish coast. I, with four hands who composed the crew, escaped in the yacht's boat, and were picked up by a passing vessel. That boat, I may as well tell you, was a lifeboat, or we must have been swamped a dozen times, for she was frequently filled, and turned over. The gale moderated shortly after, and the vessel proceeded on her way. She was bound to California for hides, and was short-handed. Our accession of force was valuable, and no means were taken to send us home by any homeward-bound ship that hove in sight. So in the course of time we arrived at our destination. After many months of toil I contrived to reach England again, and then made enquiries about the yacht, &c. All I could learn was that Clifford had survived the danger in which I left him, as well as my infant child, but that my wife was dead. No one, however, had heard anything of Clifford or Mabel for nearly two years. I could discover no clue to their whereabouts, neither could I learn what had become of the LURLINE. My present object is to find Clifford and my daughter. Can · you then tell me where they are ? ”

“ I can.”

“ Then may I request that you will do so at once.”

“ I will answer that question by another. Have you come prepared to pay me the £100 down ? That is the ‘ open sesame ’ of my lips. Without that first in my possession I decline to give you any information whatever.”

Marsden seemed taken a little aback ; but as it was pretty clear to him that the old man was not one to be easily outwitted, he replied frankly

“ To tell you the truth, I have not brought the money with me, simply because I have not yet got it myself. You remember that the reward was conditional. The advertisement stated, as clearly as words could do, that the information was to be such as would lead to an arrest. Until I have brought Clifford to book, and have recovered property which is due to me, and which he has embezzled, I shall have nothing wherewith to pay you the promised reward.”

“ Whew ——” whistled the old man, contemptuously. Then, Sir, our conference is at an end, I fear."

" Not exactly. I can place you in a witness box, upon your oath, and extort your information from you for nothing, if I choose."

" No you can't," replied the old man, smiling. " But even if you could, I have been many times in a witness box before now, and I know how to behave myself there. Besides, what would prevent my giving warning to Clifford, and sending you on a wild goose chase? I know what I am about. The man who can outwit me in a matter of this sort must come from very far north—from the pole itself."

There was a pause for some minutes. At length Marsden said

" Suppose I tell you exactly how I am situated. You may then be induced to help me."

" Do so, by all means. I will listen to you with pleasure."

" Then the simple fact is this," replied Marsden. " Clifford has forged a will, by which he has come into possession of property which ought to belong to me. His Uncle, and namesake,

Henry Clifford, had a daughter Zoe, whom I married. He died intestate, leaving no other child. Under these circumstances, the property of the deceased would go to her, and consequently to me. Clifford, the nephew, in order to prevent this, forged a will in which he constituted himself executor and residuary legatee, and in such a way as to deprive me of every farthing."

" That is bad indeed!" said Smith, " I could never have believed such a thing possible of him. A few years ago he would have been hanged for it, and now he would be transported for life. Can you prove that he has done this?"

"Very easily."

" How?"

" That is a long story."

" But I am afraid I cannot help you unless I know all the particulars," said Smith. " I advise you to tell me. My help may be worth something, for I was once in the legal profession, and have listened to many a strange tale of human frailty. You may confide anything to me with perfect safety, for our interests are sure to be identical in this matter."

" Well then, I will tell you how the case stands. Henry Clifford, the Uncle, did not exactly die intestate, as I said just now. He made a will, which was duly signed and witnessed the day before his death, but that will was afterwards lost. Young Clifford happened to have amongst his papers the lawyer's original draft of it, so he copied that cut fair, and forged the old signatures."

"That was not quite so bad," said Smith. "It was a very risky thing to do, but not dishonourable so far as intention to defraud went. Some people might think it right. But how can you prove that the will which he deposited at Doctors' Commons is a forged one?"

"Because I happen to have found the original will, and I have it now in my pocket."

"But how is anyone to know whether that or the other is the original will,—and what can it signify to you, since the bequests are the same in both? May I see it?"

"Assuredly. Here it is."

Old Smith took the document, and read it carefully through from beginning to end.

"This appears to be quite formal and straightforward," he said. "I observe that one of the witnesses is an English solicitor, then residing at Nice. Is he alive now, and could he be produced as a witness to swear to his own handwriting, so as to settle which of the two wills is genuine, and which forged?"

" He could."

" But supposing the original will to have been really lost, do you think this same witness would then be prepared to swear to the other will being a forged one?"

" I cannot say. The signatures are extremely well done, and the original will was written out by Clifford from the lawyer's draft. The testator was in the very jaws of death at the time, and the thing was done in a hurry."

" What has become of the other witness?"

" He is dead."

" There is certainly a case against young Clifford," said Smith, " though not a very good one. The lawyer's memory might be at fault."

" That might be quickened," replied Marsden, with a cunning look.

" But still I don't see how your prosecuting Clifford would benefit yourself. The two wills are the same in effect, and in both the property is so bequeathed as to cut you off from a single sou.   What was left to your wife Zoe is to go to her children at her death.   You could not touch any of it.   The yacht and the rest of the property are left to the nephew of the testator."

" But I am alive, and I am my child's natural guardian," said Marsden.

"Then you have only to show yourself to Clifford, and suggest that fact to him.   Prosecuting him for a forgery, and proving your case by the production of the real will, which is the same as the other in all its bequests, would avail you nothing.   The act would be merely one of malice, without any benefit to yourself."

"But I hate him, and long to be revenged," replied Marsden.   "He has always crossed my path, and I mean to clear him away now, once and for ever.   Besides, the mere sight of me alive, knowing what power I have over him, will terrify him into giving me any bribe I choose to name, to keep silent on the subject of his crime. As it is, he thinks me dead, and the genuine will at the bottom of the sea with me.   But I have only to show myself and say, Clifford, I have the original will in my possession, and I shall have my enemy at my feet.   Remember,—but for his forgery, I should only have to destroy this will and the whole property would become mine. For months I toiled home from abroad, inch by inch, expecting on my arrival to find myself a rich man, and behold he has forged a will! There is good cause for my revenge—and revenge is sweet."

As Marsden said this, an expression of diabolical malice crossed his features. Old Smith observed it. He had been deeply interested in the conversation, and had watched the countenance of his visitor most attentively. His impression was that the true culprit was Marsden himself. The loss of the will, and his finding it, looked very suspicious. The whole story was beginning to assume a palpable shape.

At that moment Hannah entered the room, and placed in her father's hands a letter which a man had just brought him from the post-office.

It was the letter from Clifford. Old Smith did not open it, but said to his visitor

"Will you excuse me for a few minutes? This letter is one which requires my immediate attention. Perhaps you will be good enough to leave me whilst I read and answer it."

"Then I will take a walk on the sands," said Marsden, "and return in half an hour."

"Do so. I shall then be ready to hear what you have got further to say."

Marsden departed, and left the old man to read the letter, and reflect on its contents.

The reader will remember what that letter was about. It was written in a conciliatory tone, it recognized services rendered, it proposed an annuity by way of compensation, and it contained a full and frank apology for insults offered.

It pleased old Smith extremely. It ceded to him all that he wanted. It was entirely satisfactory. He had always liked Clifford, and he now resolved to accept his offer, and become his staunch friend. Besides, Marsden was evidently a villain,—whilst Clifford's act, although illegal, might be regarded as done in self-defence. At any rate, old Smith was not one to be too nice in his criticism on such a point,—although he could moralise at times with any right reverend lord bishop, or learned judge upon the bench.

To return to Marsden. While he was at Southampton, and as soon as he had received a letter from Jersey in answer to his advertisement, he concluded, naturally enough, that the LURLINE had been cast ashore upon the coast of that island. The first sight of the wild and desolate

Bay of St. Ouen, with its long flat sandy beach exposed to the West, made him think it probable that it was there that she had been wrecked. So he resolved to make some enquiries on the spot, before renewing his conference with Smith. When he left the cottage for a stroll upon the sands, there happened to be two men and a woman loading a cart with vraic. He therefore went up to them, and learnt, by their answers to his questions, much of what he wished to know. They told him that a yacht had come ashore there two years before—that its name was the BAGATELLE, and that of its owner John Smith— that the wife of the latter, a beautiful young creature, had been killed in the surf by a blow on the head, but that her infant daughter had been saved—also that Mr. Smith had lived in Jersey ever since, had kept his yacht at the Town Pier, and had gone a week before in her to France.

All this was information of the highest importance to Marsden. At the expiration of the half-hour he returned to old Smith's room.

"I have just learnt," he said, with an air of triumph, "pretty nearly all I wanted to know. Henry Clifford, it appears, is now in France—

that is to say, John Smith left in the BAGATELLE for France a week ago. Do you happen to know what port he went to?"

"I have not the least idea," said Smith, with perfect composure, "but that could be easily ascertained."

"Would he be safe from arrest in France?"

"I should think so."

"But if I were to charge him with stealing my yacht?"

"You would not be able to prove the charge, and the prosecution would fall to the ground. You would be saddled with the costs, and laughed at for a lunatic."

"But is there not an extradition treaty between the French and English Governments for the mutual cession of persons who have committed forgery?"

"I think not."

"Then how can I get redress?"

"Lay the case before the Lord Chancellor."

"And what will he do?"

"Prove, perhaps, that *you* stole the original will, and secreted it."

Marsden began to look angry.

"Where is the will?" he asked. "I don't see it. I left it on the bed."

"I don't know," replied Smith. "You took it with you, did you not?"

Marsden felt in all his pockets, but it was not there.

"I left it on the bed," he said. "What have you done with it?"

"I have not touched it," replied Smith. "If you have lost it, don't blame me."

"You old scoundrel!" said Marsden, perfectly livid with anger. "Give it up, or I will strangle you on the spot."

The old man fumbled under his pillow, and at length produced, not the lost will but the loaded pistol which he always kept there. It was on full-cock.

The two men glared upon each other,—but there was so much resolution in Smith's face that Marsden did not dare to attack him.

"The will has been lost, and found, and lost again," said Smith, ironically.

"And it will be *found* again," said Marsden, "if there is such a thing as a search-warrant, and a constable to be had in this place."

"It will never be found again by *you*," replied the other.

"We shall see," was the reply, as Marsden left the room.

That same day Smith's cottage was searched by a *connétable* and two *centeniers*, and every nook and corner of it thoroughly examined, but no will was found. Moreover, it was proved that no one had either been to, or left the house, since Marsden went for his walk upon the beach, except himself. The search was fruitless; and the man who had come to Jersey for his revenge had been outwitted at the first step.

Marsden went to the town, and on enquiry the next day amongst the boatmen at the harbour, learnt that the BAGATELLE had started for France a few days before, with Mr. Bell and his daughter as passengers. He then ascertained the address of that gentleman's lodgings, and on calling there was informed by Mrs. Bell that the yacht had gone to St. Malo. A steamer left for that port two days after, and in her Marsden took his passage.

The same steamer carried the mail, and in the letter bag was the following communication from Smith to Clifford, addressed Poste Restante, St. Malo.

I received your letter at a lucky moment for you, as you will find some day. I accept your proposition respecting the annuity you offer me, and will endeavour to deserve it by being your friend and looking after your interests, which are somewhat complex and require careful watching. Marsden has been here to see me. He brought a will to show me, of which, like a fool, he allowed me to gain possession. You shall see it some day—and have it if you choose. The little cottage was searched for it by three constables, but in vain.

You must keep out of Marsden's way. He is highly dangerous. There is the adder in his eye, and something of the lunatic too. He has found out much of what he wanted to know, from the people about here. He will probably cross to France after you, and worry you as long as his funds last.

I trust that the good deed which I have lately done for you will be allowed to cancel my previous perfidy,—but your rude and scornful message provoked me to it, and my destitution left me no other course.

Clifford never received the above letter. It lay in the French post-office for a year, uncalled for, and was then destroyed.

CHAPTER 18.

—

HOMEWARD BOUND—A DARING ESCAPE.

To return to the BAGATELLE :—

A river pilot boarded her at daybreak, and as it was then high water they at once passed her through the lock, and commenced rowing her down the narrow winding river, with the ebb tide. The weather was calm and hazy, with the prospect of a sultry day. Jim rowed in the bow, and the pilot aft, and at the same time directed Clifford where to steer. Kate and her Papa were both up and on deck too; and the *bonne*, having left her little charge asleep, lighted the fire for their last breakfast on board. The reaches of the river where they then were are hemmed in by rocky heights and hanging woods, and are therefore completely land-locked; so the smoke rose straight up from the little flue, and not a breath of air was felt, and not a leaf of the dense foliage on the banks seemed to stir. No one spoke—for although all were really happy, yet they could not but feel that a delightful trip was drawing to a close, and that they were bidding a long farewell to charming scenery which they might never see again, but which had become rich in associations of past enjoyment. Besides, their farewell was to the *beautiful*, and they were about to enter upon the *grand* — which is always a solemn feeling in any change of scene.

Thus, reach by reach was passed, and the banks grew lower, and the river wider, and the tide ran stronger, and a little breeze directly up the stream, and therefore against them, came on as the day advanced. This was unfortunate, as they could not tack—for that would have taken them out of the only deep channel which was practicable for the yacht—and thus their masts' and rigging held the wind, little as it was, and stopped her way, and rendered rowing and steering much more difficult. At length the river widened for a mile or two into a sort of shallow lake, and there the wind freshened and impeded them so much that in the next narrow reach they lost their tide, and had to anchor.

It was then ten o'clock, and in that spot they were constrained to lie inactive until four, when it would be high water and the tide in their favour again. But what rendered this delay more provoking was, that no sooner had they anchored than the head wind which had impeded them went down, and it became calm again. There was no help for it, therefore, but to pack up a basket of eatables, and go ashore, and while away the hours of the flood tide by a stroll. The banks were very pretty in that spot, and wooded again, and there seemed to be many winding walks about the heights,—so they went ashore in the dingey, and took another ramble in France.

The scenery of the reach of the river in which the yacht lay was a strange mixture of the inland and the marine. The water was brackish and frothy, the tide strong, the banks formed of red clay and not of rock, and the trees somewhat stunted; while through an opening might already be seen a blue line, not of sea exactly but of rocky coast. About a mile above them was a pretty little village, with a long jetty, and a fleet of sea-going craft lying within a small bay to which it afforded perfect shelter —the whole overtopped by a convent peeping out from amongst the trees.

So in due time the party went ashore—all but Jim and the pilot, who remained on board—and were landed at the little village aforesaid. Then some time was spent in rambling about the lanes, mounting to the Convent, and lastly looking over the grounds of an old Château belonging to a wealthy merchant of the neighbouring port. These extended along the heights immediately abreast of where the yacht was lying, and commanded lovely views. There they whiled away the hours until hunger came strong upon them—for dawdling about in the fresh air is hungry work—and then their basket was opened, and the prog produced. The spot chosen for their picnic was a level platform, cut in the bank above the river, and as it happened, exactly opposite the yacht. Its height above the water might be about thirty feet, and the bank, which was of clay, was quite perpendicular, except near the bottom, where it had been hollowed out slightly by the tide. Round the back of this platform a rustic seat had been put up, and a pathway led to it from the grounds above. At no great distance beneath it there was a little quay or landing belonging to the Château, and a boathouse near.

By the time that they had picnic'd it was three o'clock, and in another hour the yacht was to be under weigh again. The old clergyman, with the *bonne* and Mabel, then strolled off towards the little quay, while Kate and Clifford still lingered on their rustic seat. There they chatted, and chatted, until their talk at length was about her happy home in England—that little rectory where she had been born, and so well brought up, and to which her lover was to accompany her when her family returned.

" Now tell me," he said, " how you pass your time at home."

" Well,—you must know we all have lessons still—for Papa says that education is never finished so long as anyone has time to learn. My Aunt, his sister, whom you met in Jersey last year, teaches us. She is very clever in some things—mostly languages, history, and grammar."

" Capital. One can never know too much. Your Papa is right. I shall get her to teach

me too, and I shall join your class—may I?
I promise to be more diligent than any of you.
Perhaps I could give you a wrinkle in Italian,
for I speak it much better than I do French,
having lived in Rome and Florence so long.
But tell me, what comes next, when lessons
are over?"

"Then I am afraid I run wild until dinner
time, and go off somewhere on the grey pony,
or have a row in our boat on the canal, or see
what the old gardener is about."

"And what sort of an old fellow is he?"

"A dear old man—quite a character—and he
is our clerk as well."

"And plays the fiddle in church too, I'll
be bound."

"No, not now.   We have got a nice little
organ, and Ellen plays upon it."

"And you sing?"

"Well, I'm afraid I do sometimes—but
Mamma sings the best.   We all sit up in the
gallery.   It is such a funny dear little old-
fashioned church."

"And the prettiest little churchyard in the
world, I'll be bound,—with long wooden
tomb-*stones* I was almost going to say, with

texts of scripture on them, reminding the reader of the vanity of life. But the great people have their hatchments, and their marble tablets, and their monuments by Flaxman, and all that sort of thing, inside, hav' n't they ? "

" Yes; and last year a painted window was put up. We all did something towards it, and subscribed our mite."

"That was a pity, for I am sure it must disfigure the dear old church. I shall get up some night, and smash it, when I go."

" Oh, you rude thing—how can you say so ? It is beautiful. But look—do you see—there is a boat with some people in it, by the side of the yacht ? "

Clifford had not seen it, for he had been looking fondly in his companion's face and watching every movement of her rosy lips,—but at her remark he turned and saw the boat.

" Ah, what can they be doing ? " he said. " There are three of them—a common-looking man and two soldiers. I wonder what they want. Now, see, they 're off again, and rowing up the stream. How fast they go—the tide must be running strong yet. And now look— Jim and the pilot are beginning to hoist the

mainsail. We have only half an hour more
to stop—and then adieu to *La Belle France!*
—I shall always love it for the happiness I
have known here."

" Perhaps we had better go at once," said
Kate, rising from her seat and walking to the
edge of the platform. Clifford followed her,
and held her hand while she looked over.

" What an awful height it looks!" she said.
" Fancy if either of us should tumble over—
and how deep the water looks too—it was all
mud there when we first came."

" But now it is high water nearly, and in this
river the spring tides rise forty feet."

He picked up some large stones, and flung
them in.

" Oh, pray take care," said Kate, " don't go so
near the edge—it makes me quite giddy to see
you."

" Come then, let us sit down once more, just
for five minutes, until Jim puts off for us in the
little boat. Look—those soldiers have landed at
the village now,—and see how busy Jim is,
running out the jib, and heaving on the anchor,
all ready for a start. He's a first rate fellow,
that. I don't think the tide runs quite so fast
2 E

now. It will turn soon. One more little talk, and then we'll start."

So they sat down together for just five minutes more, as they fondly thought—but which proved to be twenty—when all of a sudden, and with cat-like noiselessness of step, the man and the two soldiers whom they had seen in the boat, and afterwards land at the village jetty, emerged from the little path and stepped upon the platform.

At that instant Clifford was looking fondly into the sweet face of his companion, and saying "And then my Katie you will be all my own."

Suddenly he felt her hand squeeze his own tightly, and her whole frame shiver. He looked up, and for an instant his blood seemed turned to ice. The man from the boat, whom he had pronounced common-looking, stood facing him, drawn up to his full height, with his arms folded, and a smile of diabolical hatred and gratified revenge upon his face!

For an instant Clifford trembled, but he recovered himself, and rose to confront his foe.

"Charles Marsden!" he exclaimed. "Alive!"

"Yes! Henry Clifford! Alive, and come to assert my rights—backed by the officers of the law. You are our prisoner."

"There was no need for this," was Clifford's mild reply. "You have but to state your claim, and all that is justly your's shall be returned, to the uttermost farthing. I have been a faithful steward, and have kept account of all that I was compelled to spend in your child's behalf. Your money and your child shall both be returned to you, when and where you like."

"But my WIFE, and my REVENGE," hissed the other, like an enraged snake. "What of them?"

"The former *you* deserted, and *I* risked my own life to save," said Clifford, sternly. "As for the latter, I can protect myself. I laugh your threats to scorn."

"Do you? Then listen. To the destitute this world is a bed of thorns, and through your infernal robbery I have been doomed to crawl upon it, on my belly, in agony, for the last two months, while you have made it a bed of down at my expense. MURDERER and FORGER! I have come for my revenge! It is your turn to suffer now, and I will have it out of you, ten times told. You prate to me of my money and my child,—you forget my deadly hatred, and the sweetness of my revenge. Murderer and Forger, you are found out at last!"

"Dare to repeat that word," said Clifford, in a tone scarcely above a whisper, but with an intensity of will, "and by the God above us, I will take you by the neck and fling you like a dead puppy into yonder stream."

"Will you?" said the other sarcastically, and at the same time drawing a pistol from his pocket, and cocking it—"Move but one step towards me, and I will drive a bullet through your heart. When I go to trap dangerous vermin I go armed."

As Marsden stood thus confronting Clifford and awaiting in mocking irony his reply, he looked a fiend in human form. He was slight and weak in frame, and his broken gait and jaded face told a tale of a constitution which had been shattered by early dissipation and recent hardship of no ordinary kind, but his hollow eye was then preternaturally lighted up like that of an adder about to spring, and there was a mocking smile upon his lip which left no hope of quarter to his hated foe. That man, in the midst of his fiendish passions, was a loathsome and an awful sight. As for his antagonist—the hot blood had mounted to his face, and there was anger in his flashing eye, but no deadly malice,—and his thoughts had already turned to some daring act by which he might escape.

At that momentous crisis Clifford looked at Kate, and beheld her eyes fixed upon him in speechless agony. "Leave me, I implore you," he whispered. "Without you to guard I can still escape. They are but three. Hurry to the boat. I will meet you there."

But she heeded not his words. She still continued looking in his face, like one petrified with horror.

"He is a liar," said Clifford to her, in a louder tone. "Believe him not. There does not crawl upon this fair earth a fouler reptile than that man."

At this, Marsden stepped aside and gave the signal to the two gendarmes to arrest their prisoner.

But the nearer of the two soldiers had scarcely moved a step towards him, when, with the speed of thought, Clifford rushed to the edge of the platform, and leaped into the river beneath!

Was that an attempt at suicide—or a desperate effort to escape? By a common impulse they all stepped to the edge to see. There could be no doubt about it. That daring act, so quickly improvised and so swiftly executed, was an attempt to escape, and brave all risks. But still the hazard was not great, and he had not miscalculated his own skill. He had leaped —as all good divers do when jumping from an enormous height—feet foremost into the water; and then, after sinking in the same position until he touched the muddy bottom, he rose quickly and struck out, as if the leap had been a mere act of sport, for the yacht, which was still at anchor in the middle of the river and in slack tide.

On seeing that his victim had thus far, at any rate, escaped his malice, Marsden presented his pistol at the swimmer, and fired; but the bullet missed. He then produced a second pistol, and was again about to aim, when one of the gendarmes called out

"Hold! That is against the law of France. I warn you not to fire. Leave that to us. It is *our* duty to arrest the prisoner, not yours."

But the warning was unheeded. Marsden fired, and this time hit his mark. A sharp cry, and presently a stain of blood upon the water, told that the swimmer had been struck,—but still he struggled on, though now with one arm only.

At that sharp cry of pain, and the sight of her lover's blood, Kate uttered a faint scream,—and then, perceiving that one of the gendarmes was raising his weapon and about to fire too, she flung herself before him, and clung to him so forcibly and so dangerously over the very edge of the platform, that the man had to retire a step or too, and drag her back. She then clapsed his knees, and would have implored him in words of agonised entreaty to spare her lover,—but the words failed her, and her eyes alone were eloquent in his behalf. The man stooped and whispered a word or two, which however she did not comprehend, and then fired—but the bullet missed. The other man also fired, and with the same result.

Clifford still swam on, despite his wound, and had more than half reached the yacht; while Jim, who had witnessed the whole proceeding, was already in the dingey and sculling towards him.

"*Sacré Cochons!*" exclaimed Marsden, in his anger, to the gendarmes. "Reload and give me your guns,—I warrant you I will hit him."

But the men pushed him contemptuously aside, and reloaded at their leisure. Their second shots were not more successful than their first, for they both missed again.

Clifford had now escaped. Jim had got safe hold of him, and was hauling him into the little boat. For the gendarmes to have fired a third time would have been against the law, for it would have put in peril the life of an innocent man.

The rage of Marsden knew no bounds. He heaped upon the gendarmes every vituperative epithet which a perfect knowledge of their language, so rich in such expressions, affords— and then added

"The scoundrel will escape! There is a breeze now in their favour, and they are all ready to start. But there is still a chance. Back to our boat, and after them. We might catch them yet. The wind may baffle them, perhaps, in one of the reaches—or they may stick on some shoal spot."

"They have a river pilot on board," answered the elder of the gendarmes, with a sneer, "and the wind is now quite steady from the south-east, and right aft. It is all plain sailing now with them. The tide has turned and they are fairly off. Nothing but a fast steamer could catch them now."

At these words Kate uttered a cry of joy,—
and then fainted in the arms of the other
soldier, who was supporting her.

"Dog!" hissed Marsden between his teeth,
to the man who had spoken last. "You shall
pay for this. I will report you to the Préfet.
I heard you whisper to her that you meant
to miss. She shall swear to it herself."

The gendarme who was thus addressed smiled
contemptuously, and touched Marsden on the
shoulder, saying in a stern voice

"You are my prisoner. I warned you not
to fire—I told you it was against the law—but
you took no heed. You fired with intent to
kill, and your bullet struck the man. There
are three witnesses to prove it. The case is
simple, and the law is strict and plain. You
will have to serve ten years at the galleys
for what you did just now. Come, *brave Anglais*,
you are my prisoner. Follow me at once."

"I understand you," replied Marsden. "I
was angry, and used strong words. I humbly
beg your pardon. Accept this trifle, and buy
yourself some drink."

So saying, he offered him a five-franc piece.

"François," said the gendarme to his com-
2

panion, as he held up the piece of money contemptuously between his finger and thumb. " Look—you are a witness to this bribe." And then he added, turning to Marsden, " Come Sir, you and I must go."

" Shall you want me to go with you to guard him ? " asked François.

" No. Attend to the young lady, and restore her to her friends. One man armed as I am is enough guard for him."

" He has weapons, Jean. Take care," was the reply.

" Give me your pistols then," said the gendarme to his prisoner.

Marsden flung them down ; and as his guard stooped to pick them up he took exact measure of him at all points. He was a powerful man, and well armed — for his musket had been reloaded, and his bayonet was fixed. There was no hope from a scuffle with him, nor did there seem to be a hope of escape at all; but defeated malice is equal to any desperate act.

" You go first along the path," said the gendarme to Marsden, " while I follow; and be careful not to go too fast, or I promise you a bullet shall bring you to a dead halt."

·They disappeared, leaving the other soldier alone with Kate. She had recovered from her swoon, but was sobbing violently, with her face buried in her hands.

"Mademoiselle," said the man kindly, "permit me to conduct you to your friends."

"No, no—leave me—not yet—I can't go yet."

Five minutes had scarcely elapsed when they heard the other gendarme calling loudly from the path

"François — François — come here."

The latter instantly left Kate's side and hastened to the assistance of his comrade. On reaching him, at a sudden turn of the footpath amongst the bushes, he beheld a hideous sight! His brother gendarme was wiping his bloody bayonet with a tuft of grass, and Marsden lay upon the ground a corpse!

"How is this, Jean?" asked François.

"Very simple," was the reply. "His foot slipped, and as I stooped to pick him up he stabbed me twice with a long clasp knife. The blows were well aimed, but he had not strength enough to drive them home. Then, I did but point my bayonet at him in my own defence, and he rushed upon it, and it pierced him through the heart."

" Are you hurt yourself ? "

" Only a scratch, I think,—but let us see."

He pulled open his coat and shirt, and found the two wounds to be no more than he had thought. The point of the knife only had penetrated the thick clothing, and scratched the skin. The " *brave Anglais* " had been too weak to inflict a mortal wound.

The yacht was now fairly out of sight, and Clifford had escaped !

CHAPTER 19.

A TEST OF FRIENDSHIP.

As soon as Clifford had been helped on board the yacht, he was left standing by the main shrouds while Jim and the pilot got her under weigh. The latter had already hove up the anchor until it swung beneath the stem, and then it was but the work of a minute to run up the jib and forestaysail, and let her head pay off. A fine fresh breeze had sprung up from the south-east, right down the river, at the turn of the tide, and the little vessel quickly filled and made way, with her bow pointing seawards. Then the pilot took the helm, and Jim set the foresail on her, and away she went, laying over it, and bounding onwards like a thing of life. Nothing but a yacht of greater tonnage as clipper built, or a fast steamer could have caught. her. The gendarme was right in what he said. Clifford had escaped.

But what were his feelings then—wet, wounded, panting still—and left with life in him it was true, but with all that seemed to make life worth having gone? During the first rapid manœuvres with the sheets and sails he had simply got out of the way of the men, and stood aside, like one half stupified and in a dream,—but when at last the yacht was fairly off, and bearing him away, he remained with his eyes rivetted upon the platform in the bank, where *she* could still be seen. Many times he waved his hand to her, but she returned him no farewell sign—for in truth her eyes were blinded with tears, and she only saw the vessel dimly as it sailed away. But still he stood with eyes fixed upon her, until at length she dwindled to a speck,—and then a sudden turn of the river hid her from his view.

And then came the crushing thoughts that he had left her, alone and unguarded, to the mercy of his deadly foe—that he had deceived her—that he had offered her the hand of a felon—that he had blasted her young life—that her father would despise him—and that she would herself come in time to execrate his memory. He had been called a murderer and a forger, in her presence—and she must have believed it, or surely she would once at least have waved him a farewell. Such were his thoughts; and while that agony lasted it would have been a mercy to have struck him dead!

"Come, my poor lad," said Jim, touching him respectfully upon the shoulder, "Bear up—you will see 'em all again one day—don't take on—come down below with me, and let's have off your wet things, and see what's the harm done. Come—I'll be as good as a mother to you, and better than some mothers that I've know'd. Why that sweet lassie that we've left behind don't love you better than rough old Jim does. Come then—let me help you down."

A word of sympathy *at the right time* acts like balm. At its soothing cadence the racked nerves cease to ache, and the burning brain to reel under its load of grief. But the *right time* for administering this precious medicine is often quickly passed—and then it becomes an irritating poison and a deadly offence. Jim, with all his faults, had a heart, and his instincts in any matter of feeling were certain to be right. He had always liked his master, as a fine

young fellow, and that sort of gentleman of
the highest type, of which men in Jim's station
have mostly a keen appreciation,—involving as
that character does the absence of all meanness,
and the frank recognition of equality between
man and man in all essential points. Jim had
always liked his master; but since their little
quarrel, and since he had come to know that
a cloud was hanging over him, his liking had
intensified into a sort of rough affectionate
fidelity, and he had resolved to stick by him
through thick and thin. This strong affection,
which, without any offence to human nature,
may be compared to that of a faithful dog,
Jim had now an opportunity for showing.
Clifford, soothed by the good fellow's kind words
at such a moment, and conscious of their common
sense as well as kindness, went down with
him below. There he changed his wet clothes,
and Jim examined his wound.

"Why, the bullet warn't no bigger than a
pea," he said, "and the pistol no bigger than
a popgun. See, here it is—it tumbled out at
the first touch,—and the bleeding aint bad
now. I'll bind the place up tight, and we'll
let that do for a day or two till we can get a

reg'lar doctor on the job—and then—why lor', it 'll soon be all right again—it aint much to hurt—only a little leaden pill buried skin deep in the shoulder."

" Jim, you 're a rare good fellow," said his master, "and I owe you my life—for I was nearly beaten when you picked me up. Those other bullets dropped pretty close about me, didn't they? It was touch and go. But what a cowardly swab I was to hollo out when the first one struck me. I don't know what it was made me do it. It wasn't pain or funk— I think it was despair."

" Oh, gammon—don't talk like that—why the more trouble a young chap gets into the more the lassies love him—give me a woman for that—it 'll all come right again some day. But I say, Cap'n, what port are we to make for now, when we get ourselves safe out of this? Not as I think they could catch us now, if the little schooner *should* give chase— for lor', they couldn't get more than seven knots out of her anyhow,—and we 're running that now — and I think the wind 'll freshen still, and chop round more to the east'ard and nor'ard before dark."

" Jim," cried the pilot, " Come up, and haul aft all the sheets—she's on a wind now, in this reach."

So for a time Clifford was left alone in the cabin with his own thoughts.

It is in such situations as he was then placed in that the difference between mens' characters is chiefly shown. Without being weak-minded or pusillanimous exactly, some men require time to think, and form their plans, and take counsel of their friends,—whilst others, more dashing and self-reliant, make up their mind at once. The former class comprises perhaps the safest men of business, the best legal advisers, and the soundest men of science ; and if life were like a game of chess, with time allowed to think between each move, such men would no doubt win in the long run. But life is in reality more like the nobler game of whist, in which a player must be smart, and act well and promptly at the same time. Hence it is that the ready, bold, and self-reliant men are oftenest the winners in the battle of life, and always leaders in the strife. Clifford belonged · to the latter type—as proved by the boldness and dash of his escape, as well as by other incidents recorded of him in this tale.

Jim had left him but a few minutes, when he took down his writing case and penned the following lines—which he enclosed in an envelope, and addressed to the Rev. Alfred Bell, —— Terrace, Jersey.

A man whom you once called your friend is now in the mire! He would remind you of your own words—spoken one morning on the ramparts of St. Malo. For him, earth which but an hour ago was a heaven has become a hell! He supplicates you for a drop of water to cool his tongue, for he is tormented in this flame. A letter addressed to Henry Clifford, Post-Office, Vigo, will find one whom you knew in happier hours under the alias of John Smith. That poor wretch will wait at Vigo until he gets a letter from you—and until then his life will be an agony hard to bear. Should no letter come from you, then Vigo will be his last resting place—his grave!

As he folded the letter a solitary tear fell upon it—a *man's* tear! He blotted it off, but still the trace remained. There was no time to write another letter, so he let that go.

Jim now returned to the cabin.

"The wind has come short," he said, " but it don't matter—we're all right—we sha' n't have to make a tack."

"Where abouts are we, Jim?" asked Clifford.

" The Citadel of St. Servan has just hove in sight."

" Then there's no time to lose. Listen to me, Jim. You are a brave faithful fellow, and I won't insult you by asking you to leave me now, as if I thought you would—for I know you won't. But the pilot—we must put him ashore, somehow."

" Never mind he," said Jim, with a knowing wink. " We want another hand. Take him on with us, and pay his passage back."

" No, no—that won't do. Besides, I want this letter posted. We must lay-to and hail a boat—or you must put him ashore in the dingey."

Jim looked thoughtful for a minute, and then smiled grimly and replied

" I sees how the cat jumps—the letter must go, or there'll be no peace aboard. Well then, Cap'n, you must go on deck and take the helm, while we watch our chance for some ferry boat, or fishing smack, to run alongside of and drop him in,—and if we don't see none about anywhere in the roads as we slip through, why then we'll lay-to outside all, and I'll land him on Cezembre Island. A five-franc piece over and above will make all straight with him."

So the matter was explained to the pilot, that the yacht was not going to bring up at St. Malo but to stand right out to sea—and that he was to be landed the best way they could, and was to go and find the old gentleman whom he had seen aboard, and give a letter into his own hand; but that if he couldn't find him he was to put it into the post.

This being clearly understood, and a prodigious douceur added to sharpen the fellow's wits, they still cracked on upon the yacht, and looked out sharp for some means of putting him ashore. Happily a chance turned up—for a fishing boat was seen at anchor a very little out of their right course. The yacht bore down upon her under full sail, and as she dashed swiftly past, the pilot leaped from her gunwale into the boat.

The wind had by this time chopped round to the north-east, and therefore, close-hauled to it, they threaded the intricate channel of the Grande Porte—one well-known to Jim—and having passed to leeward of Cezembre and the Jardin Beacon, stood out to sea on the same tack.

In another hour the French coast had dwindled to a grey line upon the horizon, and St. Malo could no longer be discerned. Clifford and his faithful mate were alone upon the waste of waters!

CHAPTER 20.

—

OFF CAPE FREHEL.

We must follow the fortunes of those two men in the BAGATELLE. What happened in France after Clifford's escape the reader will learn in due time.

"What port are we bound for now, Cap'n?" said Jim at length—for since putting out the pilot he and his master had hardly exchanged a word.

"Vigo," replied Clifford. "Do you know the place?"

"Vigo? I'm blow'd if I ever heard of such a place. Where may that be, Cap'n?"

"It's a snug little port on the coast of Spain, not far from Cape Ortegal. I know it well. I was in there once and we stayed a week."

"Then it must be on t'other side of the Bay of Biscay, and we'll soon have to pay out more sheet, and up squaresail if the wind keeps like this—as I 'm of opinion it will, for the next week to come. See what baffling winds we 've had for the last month from the south'ard, and south-east'ard—regular calms, and Paddy's hurricanes up and down the mast. And then it always blows from the nor 'ard, or nor 'ard and east 'ard, all down that coast at this time of the year—just like being in the trades. We 'll keep this wind, I 'll bet, all the way—and that 'll be a good job, as we 're so short of hands. How many hundred miles may it be, Cap'n, to—Vigo, eh ?"

" Five or six hundred, I think, Jim,—but I must go down below now and look at the charts. You take the helm."

" Why lor', then we 'll be there in three or four days, if the weather keeps like this. My eyes, ain't she walking—why she 's doing now nine knots easy—if not ten."

" Are you glad to go, Jim ?"

" Ain't I just ? Why this is like plum pudding to me. They may hunt you about, Cap'n, all over the world, if they likes—I 'm game. This is a d——d sight better than lying in the mud of St. Helier's harbour all one's life.

Something to do, and something to think on
—that's what I like."

"What provisions and water have we got
aboard, Jim?"

"Lots—don't you fash about that—enough
to last us two till Michaelmas. I never puts to
sea on short allowance—trust me for that."

Clifford now went below, and Jim took
the helm.

He looked round the cabins—and first at that
in which he and Mr. Bell had slept. There
was the kind old gentleman's luggage, just
as he had left it when they started for their
walk—some things lying about, the rest neatly
put away. What would he do without it?
Then he turned gently the handle of the door
of the ladies' cabin, and opened it with hesitation,
as if he half thought *she* might still be there.
How neat and tidy—how beautifully clean
it was—*her* berth on one side—Mabel's on
the other—and the *bonne's* athwartship. Everything in order, and nicely put away, all but
certain little slippers, and gloves, and a straw
hat, and one of Mabel's toys, and the *bonne's*
funny Breton white cap. He looked round
on all this, but touched nothing,—and then

resolutely retreated, as if it was profanation for him to remain in such a spot. He closed the door and locked it and put away the key, saying to himself as he did so "Not a soul shall enter that cabin again until *she* does—that I swear." Then he spent some minutes looking at the charts—and then he went on deck again.

"We'll go through the Race of Brehat, Jim, and inside the Roches Douvres, and inside the Seven Islands too, in sight of the French lights. They'll be a comfort to us in the night," said Clifford.

"And the nearest course too," said Jim, "and by to-morrow morning at daylight we'll have passed the Isle' de Batz."

"Let us keep all standing, Jim, and carry on upon her till the crack of doom. I can work and do my share. I've got one arm good. Blow, St. Antonio, blow, and drive us quickly on. It warms the blood."

He took the helm again. Jim slacked off all the sheets a bit, and they went a little more off the wind, and changed her course a point. Then he dived below, and came up presently with a black bottle in his hand.

"I never thought of this here comforter before," he said. "If any chap had told me that, I'd have said he was liar to his face. Come Cap'n, take a glass—it'll do you good—you wants it, my poor lad, if ever a fellow did. Will you have something to eat too?"

Clifford smiled. Natures like his are never long depressed—and a downright friend by your side in trouble, no matter in what station, is inspiring — and if to this comfort there be added something to be done and thought of, together with rapid change of scene, and the swift motion of a sail, or a gallop, or a drive, the demon of melancholy has soon to spread his dark wings and make way for hope. So Clifford positively smiled.

"Well Jim, since you press it on me with such bewitching eloquence, perhaps I *could* eat a bit if I tried—and you could too, my faithful fellow—so bring up something and let us buckle to, here on deck."

The reader must not be shocked if he is told that the result of that experiment was a complete success. They both made a hearty meal, and grouted it with a bottle of Mr. Bell's best port.

When that was over they began to chat again.

"Now Jim," said Clifford, "you must tell me all you know about my affairs. You must keep nothing back, because that would be no kindness now. I want to know first what those men in the boat said to you when they went alongside, in the river."

"Well now, that I can't tell you, Cap'n, for I don't understand much of their lingo, although I've been so many years knocking about on this here coast. It was the pilot who spoke them, and the soldiers who asked; the other man didn't say a word. I expect he told 'em all they wanted to know, and that was just where you'd gone ashore. I guessed what they wanted, and I'd have sent 'em on a wild-goose chase—only I hadn't half a chance."

"Had you ever seen that man before, Jim?"

"Never, Cap'n. On my soul I never had."

"Then how could you guess what he wanted?"

"Well then, I'll tell you all about it. Do you remember my gammoning of you about that notice in the paper, the night before we started on the trip? Well then—here it is."

He took out of his tobacco box the advertisement which he had folded up and put there for safety a fortnight before, and handed it to his master to read.

As Clifford read it his brow grew dark again.

"You should have shown me this before, Jim."

"No I shouldn't—because I know'd that would have spoilt all your fun with the young lassie. I meant to show it you as soon as wo got back to Jersey."

"But still I can't understand on what charge Marsden could venture to arrest me in France. Surely I was safe in France—only I couldn't think of everything at once—and the galleys for life would have been a sell."

"The pilot told me he charged you with having robbed him of the yacht."

"He was mad. I'm certain of it now. I was a fool not to stand my chance, and charge him with insanity, and have him locked up."

Jim made no reply; and after a pause of some minutes Clifford said, in a low tone, as if talking to himself,

"Marsden alive! What a strange thing! I could have declared I saw them all swallowed up, and the boat swamped; and Zoe saw it too. That vessel must have picked him up, and taken him abroad. Then I suppose he wrote to England, and heard the news, and worked his way home in a fury at finding his plans contravened by me. And so he swore to be revenged. I understand it now. But where could he get that hundred pounds from? I wonder if he has any friends."

There was another long pause, and then Jim said "It has been the old man's doing, all this. He peached to get the hundred pound. When you took the child away he had nothing left to live on. When you sent him back that saucy message by the boatman I know'd well enough how the affair would end."

"The old scoundrel!" said Clifford. "And yet how kind I always was to him."

"He ain't a bad old chap either, Cap'n, all round the compass. He's got some good points."

"Perhaps. Have you told me all now, Jim? Have you kept nothing back?"

"No. I knows nothing more. The old man never said a word to me about it. But shall I tell you what I've been thinking, Cap'n?"

"Yes, what?"

"Had that chap any right to fire on you? If he had that's rum law. I'm bothered if I think he had. It was the soldier's place to arrest you—not his."

"By heavens, Jim, I wish you had told me that before."

"Shall I tell you what I see'd quite plain through our big glass, just before we turned the corner and lost sight of 'em?"

"What?"

"Why, I see'd one of the red-coats trot him off. I'll swear I did—and the other one stayed with the young lassie, and led her to the seat. I see'd the man throw down his pistols and the red-coat pick 'em up,—and then the man went off first along the path, and the other followed close behind, guarding him as he went."

"Ha! Did you see that? Are you quite sure?"

"Well, a fellow can't always be quite sure at half a mile off—but it looked deuced like it."

"Shall we put back, Jim? I've half a mind," said Clifford."

"No, no,—dash it, don't put back—let's keep

on to where we're going, I say—out of England, and out of France. Then the young lassie will write to you there, and you'll soon know for certain how it all was—and then you can do what you like. Don't go and jump into a trap with your eyes shut—go easy—there's lots of time. If they nabbed him they'll keep him fast enough—you may be sure of that."

"Perhaps you're right," said Clifford. "Now Jim, you take the tiller, and I'll go for'ard and have a spy. I thought just now I caught sight of Brehat Light."

At the thoughts of the young lassie, and the red-coat leading her to the seat, Clifford's heart was full again to overflowing. He could stand no more. He went for'ard in order to be alone.

They were then abreast of Frehel Light, and about ten miles to the nor'ard of it. It was getting dusk. Clifford flung himself along the deck by the windlass, and lay with his head resting upon his arm, and that upon the rail, gazing mechanically on the receding coast, and the tall slender lighthouse, looking like a pencil stuck into the highest point of a steep bluff. Presently he saw it dart a brilliant flash— the first it gave that night. The men had

just lighted the revolving lamp, which they
always do at sunset, as he well knew. He
therefore turned and looked the other way,
and saw in the nor'west the sun's red disc
just sinking in the sea. He watched the solemn
sight, and thought of the first evening of their
trip when *she* had watched it with him, on
the Grand Bey. He struggled with his feelings,
but in vain. He could contain himself no
longer. He laid his face upon his sleeve,
and—yes, the truth must positively be told—
that proud, strong, high-spirited young man
absolutely wept!

CHAPTER 21.

—

THERE would be nothing to amuse the reader in the log of the trip of those two men in the BAGATELLE to Vigo, for happily it was a plain sail all the way, and without exciting events. The wind continued fair and steady the whole time, and for a week after, as Jim had prophesied it would; and they had a singularly quick run. On reaching their destined port they were, however, greatly fagged from want of sleep during their long and anxious watches; but before Clifford would take a moment's rest, after casting anchor in the roads, he must needs go to the post-office to enquire for a letter, and leave his address-card—although, as Jim told him, they had far outstripped the mail, and he could hear nothing for at least a week.   But notwithstanding the sound logic of their having taken the shortest cut and gone at nine knots an hour all the way, he was grieved to find no letter, and returned on board with leaden steps and a heavy heart. There are few worse tortures in life than to be disappointed of a letter when your fate seems to hang on that reply. His shoulder too was still very painful, and the day after their arrival he went to a doctor and had it dressed. On that day also no letter for him arrived. How he cursed the weary hours from day to day.   The heat also was oppressive : and once he imparted to Jim, in a moment of unusual confidence, that he felt like a caged wild beast, and that if no letter came for him within a week he should put an end to his hateful existence.   At which Jim grinned, and said, that if a sweet young girl like Miss Kate should pretend to be vexed with his master, he, Jim, would go to her himself—even if he had to trudge barefoot and beg all the way—and hear from her own lips the reason why.

Happily these dreadful threats of what they both would do had no need of being put to the crucial test, for at last the long hoped-for letter came. On the fourth day after their arrival, the post-office official handed to Clifford, with a smile, a long narrow note, rose colour, addressed to him in a pretty ladies' scrawl. How his hand trembled as he took it, and how his heart beat as he walked swiftly off with it to a leafy solitude on the promenade, and broke the seal.

But the envelope contained no letter after all! Oh, what cruelty of Kate! There was nothing in it but a little pencil sketch in outline,—and what could that possibly mean? It was a copy by her, from memory, of part of one of his own sketches which he had taken, with her seated by his side, on one of their happy days together, and had given her on their last evening at Lehon, with the others in the book. There was, of course, some deep meaning in her sending him this—but what? The original was a simple little bit enough, but in her copy much of that had been suppressed. Her outline simply consisted of a distant line of coast, with a lighthouse at one end, while in the foreground there was a stranded fishing lugger, with an anchor hanging from the bow. That was all. What could it possibly mean? Can the reader guess? Clifford was not long in doing so. The stranded lugger he thought meant himself; the anchor meant hope; and the lighthouse meant her constancy to him, and watchful care in trouble, and a star in the darkness of his night. Poetical perhaps, and far-fetched, but that was what he thought it meant.

But was it not cruel of her not to have enclosed him a single line—not a word—not half a word—not even a letter which she might have put upon the stern of the boat without the least charge of impropriety? And after he had taken that dreadful leap, and had been shot at six times, and wounded, and insulted, and chased for dear life; and when he had so often waved his hand to her at parting—and all! So he thought, or fancied he thought; but still it was exquisite to know that she had written to him at all, and that her message suggested hope—for every one has heard of the anchor of hope. There could be no mistake as to what the anchor meant.

He told Jim that a letter had come at last from the "young lassie," and that they must wait for further news; but with true delicacy of feeling he did not tell him what the letter really was. Then followed more days of anxious waiting and suspense. The place, however, was new to Jim, and he had picked up some pals on board an English collier there, and seemed happy enough. So, as Clifford preferred to stay on board all day, except at the hour when the post came in, Jim had plenty of time to stroll about, and he at least was as contented as could be under the trying circumstances of the case.

But the days hung heavily on Clifford's hands, and his old hobbies of reading and painting afforded him no relief, for his mind would not bend or yield to any other thought than that which eternally oppressed it. At last he began to chafe bitterly at not hearing again from Kate, or receiving any reply from her Father in answer to the lines which he had written to him on that hated afternoon.

It was the tenth day of this harrowing state of things. He went to the post-office, as usual, for his letter, but found none; and then he took his customary stroll round the promenade on his way back to the yacht. He was quite alone there, for the heat happened to be at its maximum just then, and everyone was in doors except himself. It was that time of day when foreigners tell you that dogs and Englishmen are the only living objects to be seen about. The solitude of that public walk, so gaily thronged at a later hour, was then complete; and he seated himself on a bench under a shady tree, with the pretty roadstead spread out before him, and the parched hills, and the coppery sky,—and communed thus with himself:—

"Why do I go on like this from day to day, fretting, and chafing, and wearing myself out? Will they write, or will they not? Kate will not—that I think is certain now. But will her Father? Yes, I think he will. But why then doesn't he? Perhaps he is making enquiries about me first. It must be so. Then I must wait, wait, wait, as I said I would. But if they only knew how cruel it is of them. If they could but see me here, for one dreary day and night, and feel all that I feel. Oh, what a hideous penalty this is to pay for what I did. And yet I thought it justifiable—why not? Well then, I shall hear from Mr. Bell some day—if only to tell me what has become of Mabel, and what steps Marsden took after I got off. I am certain to hear from him some day. But things can't go on like this. Shall I do something to try and pass away the time? I will—but what?

Let me think. Society, amusements, fishing—all would be a bore. Country walks or rides—no, it's too hot for that. Suppose I learn Spanish. That's a bright idea. Thank God for that. I will. I will begin this very day. I will buy a dictionary, and a grammar, and an exercise book as I go back,—and work hard at it, and show *her* one day all that I have done. That's capital. What folly to be idle. It is idleness that makes this torture ten times worse."

With the above good resolution he returned to the town, and looked about for a bookseller's shop where he could buy a dictionary and grammar of the Spanish language. He walked at a brisker pace, and seemed all of a sudden to have become quite an altered man, at the thoughts of a new hobby and something to do.

As he went through one of the principal streets in search of a book shop, it suddenly occurred to him that he had just passed one with the blind down. On turning quickly to retrace his steps, he caught a momentary glance of a young lady who was standing at an open window opposite, but who, on perceiving that she had been observed by him, immediately withdrew within the room. Her face and figure, thus momentarily seen, were marvellously like his Kate's ; and the thought that it might really be her come to see him, with her Papa, almost made him stagger. For a minute or two he stopped, and watched the now vacant window to see if she would return—but she did not ; then he looked more closely at the house, and perceived that it formed part of an hotel, and that the words " English spoken here" were painted upon a blind. This confirmed him in his impression that the young lady was really Kate,—and with a beating heart he entered the lobby to enquire. An English waiter presently appeared, and the following dialogue ensued :—

" I have just seen a lady at an upper window of this hotel, whom I think I know," said Clifford. " Can you inform me whether a young English lady and her father are stopping here now ? "

" I will ask the landlord, Sir," was the man's rather cautious reply.

In a few minutes he returned.

" No, Sir. There are no English stopping here now, answering to that description."

" Are you quite sure of that ? "

" The landlord has himself told me to say so."

" Thank you," said Clifford ; and as he walked away he mechanically took the turning towards the Quay. The dictionary and the grammar were forgotten. He had seen a vision which put all but one idea completely out of his head. On reaching the water side he found the dingey there, with a boy belonging to the collier left in charge of her.

" Where's Jim?" he asked.

" Gone ashore to look for you, Sir."

" Well, put me on board the yacht, my lad, and then you can come back here again."

The boy did so. As Clifford stepped upon the lonely deck of the BAGATELLE he felt dejected and sick at heart, and leant across the main boom, with his face upon his arm.

He remained thus for about five minutes, little dreaming that someone had in the meantime come up from the cabin, and was standing behind him. That someone at length touched him lightly on the shoulder. He turned, and beheld the Rev. Mr. Bell !

Clifford held out his hand to him at once, in a transport of joy, but his old friend drew back and would not take it. Then, for a full minute, the two stood facing each other, while neither of them spoke. At last Clifford could endure this no longer, and said, in accents trembling with agitation

" Speak Sir,—speak, I conjure you. Have you come here as my friend—or as my foe ?"

" I have come," was the reply, " to hear your story of yourself from your own lips; or, if you prefer it, to read it from your own pen —and that in order that I may decide what had best be done for my child's welfare. You told me once that you had written out that narrative, and that it was then on board the yacht. If it is so now, may I see it ?"

The manner in which this was said was not exactly cold, but neither was it kind or reassuring. Clifford was much hurt, and replied with the same formality

" It is on board still, Sir, and you may see it if you choose."

" Then please to go and fetch it."

Clifford went into his cabin, and in a few minutes returned with a little volume, secured by a lock and key. He handed it, with the key, to Mr. Bell.

" May I take it away with me, and read it

this evening at my leisure?" enquired the latter.

"By all means. Take it, and return it whenever you think fit. There is nothing there which I do not really wish that you should see."

Mr. Bell took the volume, and as he did so said

"Now answer me, Henry Clifford, on your honor. Is this all strictly true? Can I depend upon every word of it?"

At this question Clifford's pride was thoroughly aroused, and he was about to make an angry reply, but he checked himself, and resolved to keep his temper—a thing which *any* one can do under *any* circumstances, if he will only take the trouble to try.

"On my honor then," he replied, "every word of that document is true. There is neither exaggeration, nor false coloring, nor malice in any part of it. It is all plain simple matter of fact, to the best of my knowledge and belief."

"You assert this on your honor," replied Mr. Bell. "But do you know what honor means? It is just that question which I have come here now to solve. May I tell you what *I* think about it? It is that honor is a moral quality characteristic of the higher races of mankind, and lying at the basis of their higher civilization. Without honor we English should sink to the level of the Asiatics. A certain state of civilization is compatible with universal lying—as you may see by reference to the Chinese, the Japanese, and the Malays—but unless, as a rule, a man can put faith in the word of his fellow, no state of society above that is possible. Hence, a man of a higher type who has no sense of honor, or who knowingly breaks any law of his country, is a traitor to the civilization from which he derives many inestimable benefits."

After a pause of some seconds Clifford looked imploringly in the face of his old friend, and said, with passionate earnestness

" Why do you torture me ? Why are you so cold—so stern ? Have you only come here to insult me ? Have I waited here through days and nights of agony for this ? I could not have believed it of you ! If this is a right result of your higher civilization, then the Pariah and the savage shall be my friends in future, and not the white man."

To this Mr. Bell made no other reply than to request that he might be put ashore at once.

Clifford therefore hailed the boy, and in a few minutes the dingey was alongside. Mr. Bell stepped into it, without taking Clifford's hand, and the boy pushed off.

" And this is friendship!" muttered Clifford in a low tone, but loud enough for Mr. Bell to hear.

He replied—"It is; the truest, the most devoted friendship—as I trust you may live to admit, one day."

" May it prove so!" replied Clifford.

The boy in the dingey was now told to push off,—but as the lad was in the act of doing so, Mr. Bell remembered that he had made no absolute appointment with Clifford for another meeting.

" Stop," he said; and turning to the latter added "I shall read this narrative to-night, and I will come on board and see you again to-morrow morning at nine o'clock, if that hour will suit you."

" Name your own time," said Clifford. " All hours are now alike to me."

" Then nine o'clock let it be. Expect me at that hour. I will not keep you in suspense."

And thus they parted!

CHAPTER 22.

—

NARRATIVE OF A CRIME.

WHEN Mr. Bell had been put ashore, he wandered into a shady secluded spot in the suburbs of the town, and there read over many times the manuscript which Clifford had put into his hand, and which was as follows :—

HENRY CLIFFORD'S CRIME,

Narrated by Himself.

My Father's name was George Clifford. He had an only brother, Henry Clifford, and no sisters. I was named Henry, after my Uncle. The two brothers were on the Stock Exchange. I was an only child; and my Uncle had an only child, a daughter named Zoe, five years younger than myself. Both our mothers died when we were very young, and my Father

died when I was ten years old. He was then
a poor man, having recently lost a good deal
of money in a speculation. My Uncle, on the
other hand, was very comfortably off. The
two brothers were extremely attached; and
when my Father was on his death bed, my
Uncle promised him to take charge of me, and
bring me up and provide for me, the same
as if I had been his own son. This promise
he faithfully kept.

Zoe and I lived together in the same house,
more like brother and sister than cousins; and
when we grew up neither of us dreamt of
falling in love with the other, although as
relations we were very much attached. I was
educated at a public school, and Zoe by a
governess at home. When I left school I
wished to be an artist, so my Uncle sent me
to Italy, in order that I might study there;
and on my coming of age he allowed me
£200 a year. I was very fond of my studies,
and worked hard. About the time of my leaving
school my Uncle gave up business, and retired
upon his fortune. He bought a yacht, named
the LURLINE, which he kept at Nice, Spezzia,
&c., and spent much of his time in Italy. Zoe

and her governess always accompanied him. Whilst I was following my studies in Rome and Florence, I often saw my Uncle, of course; and sometimes took a cruise with him. We were at that time a very united family. I liked my Uncle extremely, and he was very kind to me, and treated me like a son. I have sometimes thought that he wished to see me married to Zoe. She grew up a beautiful girl, but *petite*. In her way she was quite a litte genius, very imaginative and romantic, with an affectionate heart, and an impulsive temper. Her Father was dotingly fond of her.

Now begins the sad part of my story.

Zoe made in Florence the acquaintance of a man named Marsden, whom both her father and I detested, as a snob. He had been an actor, and was a poor devil, a *vaut rien*, and an unprincipled dissipated fellow, much older than herself, and without either talent or good looks. What she could see to like in him no one could conceive. Her Father, although kind as a man could be, was firm, and had a will of his own. He would not hear of her marrying the scamp; so the end of it was that she eloped with him. This only made matters worse between herself and her father. He refused to recognise the match, or to have anything to say to her husband; but at the same time he offered her a home again if she would be separated from him. At the end of two months she consented, and returned to her father's house. During that time she had lived in a state of poverty and misery, and had begun to be ill-treated by her husband, since he discovered that her father was inexorable, and would not advance him any money for her support. All this preyed upon my Uncle's mind, and brought on an attack of illness, from which he never recovered. At last little Mabel was born; and about a year after that my Uncle died. In the meantime Marsden had disappeared. No one knew what had become of him, except his wife; for they, as she afterwards confessed to me, had occasionally corresponded.

The day before my Uncle died, he had an old will destroyed, and a new one made. This happened at Nice. He had become very suddenly worse, and an English Solicitor residing there was sent for to make the will.

The dying man called us all around him, and with perfect intelligence, although in feeble accents, expressed to us briefly his wishes in regard to the distribution of his property after his death. To his daughter Zoe he left the interest of £15,000 during her life, and the principal to be equally divided amongst her children at her death. To me he left the remainder of his property, including of course the yacht, and worth perhaps as much more. He appointed me sole Executor of his will. The lawyer took notes and wrote out a draft, which he read to the old man. It was approved of, and left to me to copy out fair upon a sheet of foolscap paper, whilst the lawyer left for half an hour in order to keep another equally pressing engagement. On his return, my copy was read to the dying man, and he signed it, in presence of the lawyer and his clerk as witnesses. My Uncle died the following day.

He was hardly cold in his grave before Marsden turned up again, and was received by his wife into favour. Shortly after, we all started together in my yacht for England, taking the will with us, in order that I might perform my part as Executor. We sailed from Nice to Narbonne, and there entered the Canal du Midi, in order to avoid going round by the Straits of Gibraltar, as Marsden hated the sea. We were towed to Bordeaux, and there set sail again for England. During this trip my antipathy to Marsden revived and increased, for he appeared to be a thoroughly selfish bad-hearted man; besides which, he chose to let me see that he could be jealous. In fact, we hated each other. On leaving Bordeaux, Marsden discharged Mabel's nurse, who had accompanied us thus far—which I thought an unfeeling proceeding. We had then four working hands on board. I navigated the vessel myself.

When we had arrived almost within sight of the English coast, a violent gale came on, in which we carried away our foremast. There was nothing to be done then but to lay-to at the mercy of the winds and tides. One night, during the middle of the storm, a strange moaning noise was heard. This was familiar to one of the sailors, as proceeding from a cavern in a detached rock called the Wolf, lying within sight of the Land's End. Shortly after, the rock itself was made out, with the sea breaking over it. We were drifting straight upon it. There was a heavy sea running at the time. The danger we were in appeared to be imminent.

The yacht had one boat, built according to a plan of my Uncle's, so as to right itself in any sea, if upset, and never sink. It had four thwarts for the rowers, and a seat in the stern. It could therefore hold five. The men considered the yacht doomed, and proposed to launch the boat; so it was slung from the davits all ready to let go. At this time Marsden was below, and I had been on deck for some hours. There were six of us on board, besides Zoe and Mabel. Presently Marsden came up, and then displayed in perfection the brutal selfishness of his nature. I will not describe the scene which occurred. Out of eight persons five only could be taken in the boat. The three who remained in the yacht were Zoe, Mabel, and myself. The others left us to our fate. I am glad to be able to say that of those four sailors not one was English. Three of them were Italians, and the fourth French.

By a special Providence, as it almost seemed,

tho yacht drifted clear of the Wolf, and as the wind had veered round to the nor'west we had then a hundred miles of sea-room to leeward.

With her foremast gone she laid-to beautifully. I felt that we were comparatively safe for some hours, unless the wind should shift.

As for the boat, that seemed to come to grief. Once, if not oftener, I could declare that I saw it completely swallowed up—but it rose again; and once I heard Marsden's agonised cry for help. The night was so dark, however, that it was impossible to see what the fate of those five men might be. I gave them all up for lost. I had not a shadow of doubt of it. Once, in the thick darkness, I thought I saw the form of a vessel near, but could not be quite sure. At daybreak the English coast was still in sight, and as I thought dangerously near, but the wind was rather off shore. The tide, however, was running up strong, and I feared might drift us into the dreaded race of Portland. After due consideration of what had best be done, I formed the rather daring plan of setting the spitfire jib upon her as a main-staysail, and trying to make the island of Jersey, which I had once visited in a yacht, and which

I knew could be safely approached with the wind from nor'west. This would, at any rate, be less dangerous than lying where we were; and as Jersey was completely under our lee, and a stiff nor'wester blowing, I hoped to reach it before dark. So the spitfire was set, and I stood for some hours at the tiller, with Zoe frequently by my side. That was a day never to be forgotten! The yacht flew before the hurricane at a prodigious pace, until at length bang went the sail into a thousand tatters, and she broached to! For the rest of that day we drifted at the mercy of the gale, and until the middle of the next night. The wind then suddenly moderated, leaving the tortured sea to rock itself to sleep. At daybreak I perceived a line of coast just under our lee. The tide seemed bearing us swiftly towards it. A dangerous crisis was evidently approaching. The yacht drew nine feet of water. If she struck at a distance from the shore, how were Zoe and Mabel to be saved—for we had no boat?

There was still a little breeze, setting straight on to the land; and as the daylight increased I could see that we were nearer to the coast than I at first thought. A heavy surf was breaking on the beach. I set the largest jib on her, between the main and the stump of the foremast, but it did no good, for the wind was dead on the shore, and very little of it. Then I let go the best bower anchor; it held for scarcely a minute, for the cable snapped. The second bower shared the same fate. I had then done my best, and all I could do. We were on a lee-shore, without a chance of getting off. I could see people running down to watch us, but they did not launch a boat, or apparently take any steps to help us. There was a tremendous surf. I have never seen anything like it. I knew the land for the west coast of Jersey.

I went to Zoe, and tied a life belt tightly round her, and rolled up Mabel in several folds of flannel which I secured with a piece of line. Then I stripped myself ready for a swim, all but a pair of bathing drawers, and canvas slippers. My hope was that I could push them both before me, and get ashore. A forlorn hope perhaps, but it was our only chance. The reader of these lines must believe me when I say that my only thought then was for their safety. I never once thought of my own as distinct from theirs.

We went on deck. The yacht lay rearing and curvetting to the heavy rollers which passed under her, with her head to the sea, or else any one of them must have swamped her. As near as I could judge she would touch the ground in about ten minutes, and then would come our struggle for life or death. I was perfectly calm, and Zoe's fine animal spirits and natural pluck supported her. At that awful moment she thought of the will. I went down to see for it. On going to my desk, where I had kept it locked up, I found that burst open, and the will gone! This I knew to be Marsden's doing; and I had then very little doubt that he had all along intended to steal the will and destroy it, in hopes that the whole of my Uncle's property would thereby become Zoe's, and consequently his. At any rate the will was gone! It happened, however, that the draft of the will had not been destroyed, and that I found in another desk. I put it into an empty wine bottle, together with some bank notes, and corked them up. Then I wrapped some cloths round the bottle, and jammed it into a safe place between the ceiling and the outer planking.

When I went on deck again, I told Zoe what

had happened to the will. Her reply consisted of the last words she spoke on earth. I shall never forget them. She said

" That was Charles's doing. `May God forgive him ! Henry, when it comes to the struggle in the water, don't trouble about me, but save my child. Save *her*—and if I am drowned, and you two escape, swear to be a father to her always, as mine always was to you."

I took the oath, and we embraced.

At that moment the heel of the sternpost gave its first bump upon the sand, and the bow began to slew round. The next sea hove her broadside to the surf. A man on the shore then shot an arrow at us, with a line attached. I caught the line, and fastened the bight of it to Zoe's belt.

The scene which followed has been already related in the local papers, and it is too painful to repeat.

When the yacht was left high and dry at low water, I found the bottle safe—as I had no doubt it would be. But previously to that, I had partly formed my plans about the will. It is my nature to decide quickly, and act promptly in any matter; so that, extraordinary as it may seem, I had made up my mind, even whilst carrying Mabel in my arms to the cottage, to say that I was her father, and that Zoe was my wife. I also determined to assume an *alias*, and to give a false name to the yacht. In the course of some conversation I had with old Smith, an hour or two afterwards, I called myself John Smith, and the yacht the BAGATELLE.

During the next few days I considered carefully what I had better do in the matter of the will. I understood but little of law, and took a common sense view of the case, assuming that Marsden had been drowned. I reasoned thus: If I let things take their course, the whole of my Uncle's property will become Mabel's, and I shall be left entirely destitute,—which, if my Uncle were alive, he would be very grieved to see. Suppose it were possible, I said to myself, that his spirit could return to earth, and advise me what to do, what advice would it give? Clearly, I thought, to carry out his own wish and intention with respect to his property, and not to act like a coward and give up my own rights, for the sake of a mere sentimental scruple. Then again, I reflected that I had sworn to Zoe to act

like a father to her child always; but how could
I do this with any good effect, so long as I was
myself destitute of all resources, and she possibly
with another guardian appointed by law? These
considerations suggested to me the forging of a
new will, exactly like that which had been stolen;
and they seemed to render such an act justifiable
under the circumstances, although illegal. On
the other hand, it occurred to me that I might
still retain my rights, without breaking the law,
thus: I might state, before the proper legal
authorities, that the original will had been
stolen; and in support of my statement I might
obtain the evidence of the lawyer at Nice, to the
effect that the original will had been properly
signed and witnessed; that he had himself seen
it after my Uncle's death; and that the draft
of it which still existed was the same, word for
word, as the original will.

Such were the considerations on which I had
to form my conclusion as to how I ought to act.
Nothing could be simpler, on the one hand,
than to make another fair copy from the draft
of my Uncle's will, and to imitate the old
signatures; while on the other hand, putting
the matter into Chancery would involve much

expense, delay, and the risk of an adverse verdict. Therefore, knowing, as I said before, nothing of law, and being unable to foresee what course the law might take in the matter, I resolved on taking the law into my own hands. I forged a new will precisely like the old one; so like it, in fact, in all respects, that I doubt whether the witnesses themselves would have been able to tell which was which, if the two had been laid before them side by side.

Next, when I came to consider what I had done so hastily in changing my name, and calling myself Mabel's father, it appeared to have been an unwise and unnecessary proceeding, of which I half repented. But still, when I considered that there was just a chance of Marsden having escaped with life, I resolved to adhere to my *alias*, as a measure of precaution—at any rate for three or four years. Subsequent events have proved that it was fortunate that I did so.

I went to London shortly after Zoe's funeral, and transacted the business connected with the will, and the Executorship. The whole of my Uncle's property became then at my own disposal.

On my return to Jersey I maintained my *alias* of John Smith. I had the yacht repaired and refitted in the old style, and for many months lived entirely on board. Mabel I left in charge of Hannah Smith.

For a long time I was very unhappy. I soon felt that I had made a grievous mistake in breaking the law of my country; and I would gladly have given every penny of my fortune to recover my lost innocence and self-respect. But repentance was unavailing, and as nobody had been wronged by my act I was denied the luxury of reparation. There were times also when, as I lay in my narrow berth at midnight, the thoughts of Marsden being possibly still alive, and returning one day with the stolen will as evidence against me, would haunt my fancy until I could endure it no longer, and I had to get up and dress myself, and walk upon the Pier until daybreak.

Thus time wore on. Marsden returned not, and my spirits recovered by degrees their tone and elasticity. I felt safe. The past began to fade from my mind and the future to look bright. A year after I had been in Jersey I made the acquaintance of Miss Catherine Bell, then a lovely girl of sixteen. She came over to Jersey for a few months on a visit to her Aunt. That was a year ago. In a hundred ways we met, though not at her Aunt's house, and a new hope filled my heart. She left in the Autumn, but it was to return with the rest of her family in the Spring. They came. At the Club I met her Father. He was a man whom I soon began greatly to like and respect, and we were much together. I longed to be introduced by him to his wife and daughters, and to visit them at their own home, but that happiness was for some reason or other always deferred; and then I began to hear that vague rumours were whispered about me in the island. It was reported that I had no friends in England, nor relations; that I had come to Jersey without letters of introduction; and that a mystery of some sort enveloped me in connexion with the Yacht. It was said also that the inscription on Zoe's tombstone was peculiar and equivocal, and that Mabel did not in the least resemble me. I know now that the originator of these rumours was my man Jim. He had discovered the name LURLINE carved upon a beam in the forecastle of the yacht; and had also found a letter of Marsden's, which I had picked up on the shore on the day of the wreck, and had left in the pocket of his overalls which I wore that day—and which letter contained an allusion to Zoe and Mabel as being Marsden's wife and daughter, not mine. I do not, however, blame Jim for any bad intention in spreading these reports; but men in his station will talk,—aye, and persons who ought to know better also.

At length I took a bold step, for Mr. Bell's visit to Jersey was drawing to a close. I invited him and his family to a sail and picnic in the yacht. To my delight the invitation was accepted. The next morning, however, I had a dispute with Jim, who was getting tired of his idle life; and I went to tell old Smith about it. At that interview I learnt that he knew enough about me to render my residence in Jersey any longer impossible, and perhaps even to cause me to be arrested on mere vague suspicions. We quarrelled. I took away Mabel, and resolved to leave Jersey at once. That night, impelled by the sudden change in all my plans, I confessed my love to Kate, and was not refused. The next morning she and her Father accompanied me to France in the BAGATELLE.

On the last afternoon of our trip, Marsden suddenly appeared before me! He charged me with murder and forgery! I was thunderstruck, and at the moment thought only of how I could escape. I have since learnt, however, that the ground of my attempted arrest was simply the less formidable and very absurd charge of his, that I had stolen his yacht; a charge which he could not have proved, and which must have ended in my release and his discomfiture. I have also learnt from Jim that Marsden was enabled to track me, in consequence of old Smith having given him information of my whereabouts, in answer to a recent advertisment in the Times offering £100 reward for such information.

I have nothing more to say. A friend will not need that I should add any attempt at a justification of my conduct, or any expression of unhappiness which he may have it in his power to relieve.

Such was Henry Clifford's sad tale. He had, by his own confession, actually committed forgery and perjury, which, if proved against him, might cause him to be transported for life.

Mr. Bell read the story many times. He then returned to his hotel, and in the privacy of his own room threw himself upon his knees and prayed for guidance from above, as to the line of conduct which it would be his duty to pursue in relation to all whom this terrible confession might involve.

He rose with a heavy heart and a clouded brow. He had never dreamt that things could have been so bad as this. Marsden's charge against Clifford, of having stolen the yacht, as he learnt at St. Malo, if not altogether absurd, he imagined could be cleared up and set straight, even if it did involve, as might just be possible, some youthful indiscretion. But deliberate forgery and perjury! Such crimes seemed truly awful. They could admit of no excuse. He had left St. Malo for Vigo, with his daughter, hoping, and indeed feeling certain in his own mind, from his knowledge of Clifford's honorable character, that his narrative would contain a satisfactory explanation of his conduct, or at any rate one on which a reasonable excuse might be founded,—and that a happy reunion would result, and they would return together, probably in the yacht. He had never dreamt of such a blow as this!

For several hours he remained in his own room writing letter after letter to Clifford, every one of which he tore up when he had written it, because it seemed too cruel— but every one of which was in fact a shade sterner than that which had gone before— until he satisfied himself at last; and then the lines which were to crush his poor young friend and his daughter's lover to the very dust, were resolutely folded up and sealed.

During all those weary hours Kate had been left in a state of suspense, it is true, but she had been shown the way to a sort of summer-house upon the roof of the building, which commanded a view over the Harbour, and there she had amused herself with a telescope, watching the manœuvres of the boats and ships, but especially the BAGATELLE,—little dreaming of the sorrow which was in store for her that night!

At length her Father joined her. He put Clifford's manuscript into her hand, and said to her, in a voice thick and scarcely articulate through emotion

" Take this, dear child, to your own room, and carefully read it through. I will come to you by - and - bye, and tell you then what I mean to do. May we both be supported through this heavy trial!"

Kate took the manuscript with trembling hands, and descended with it to her own room. Her Father's manner left no room for doubt. Poor Clifford was in deep disgrace!

For more than three hours that night, her lover paced backwards and forwards before the window of the Hotel, at which he had no doubt then that it was Kate whom he had seen in the afternoon. There was a light burning in the room, as he could perceive through the jalousie blind, but no one seemed astir. She might have gone to bed, weary with her tedious land journey of a thousand miles through dust and heat, from St. Malo; or she might be reading his narrative of his crime. He thought most probably the latter; and still he waited on,—and was repaid at last. Her shadow was suddenly cast across the blind, and then that was thrown back, and she looked out from the open window. With instinctive delicacy he remained in the shadow of a wall for a few moments, and watched her. She did not look up and down the street as if in search of any one, but simply came to the window to breathe the night air and cool her brow. She had not begun to undress, and yet it was past midnight. He could not see her features distinctly, but there was in her attitude a sort of melancholy unconsciousness and reverie. At length he stepped forth into the middle of the street, took off his hat, and stood before her.

She did not acknowledge him—she made him no sign—she did not move—she stood like a figure suddenly turned to stone—with her eyes fixed, not on him but on the pavement at his feet! There he stood, with beating heart—but hers it seemed had ceased to beat for him. He felt deeply hurt. At length he put on his hat again, and was about to go—with a vow to weigh anchor that night and never see her more—when just as he was leaving, her woman's heart could stand it no longer, and she waved her hand—breaking by that act a solemn promise made to her Father but a few minutes before. Clifford raised his hat in deep acknowledgement of her kindness, and was about to speak to her, but she instantly retired within the room.

CHAPTER 23.

HOPE CRUSHED—A MOMENT'S MADNESS.

CLIFFORD returned on board the yacht, undressed, and threw himself upon his berth; but it will readily be believed he could not sleep a wink that night. It was his nature to *hope*, and something seemed to tell him that his old friend's coldness was assumed—that he would be satisfied with the narrative—that he would be convinced of his, Clifford's, perfect integrity and purity of motive—and that the next day would be one of joy—of delicious reunion—of happiness which would repay him a hundredfold for what had passed—that he should clasp his Kate to his fond heart again—that all would be made up—and that they would return together in the yacht. As for Marsden, and his uncompromising revenge

—Mr. Bell, he thought, would become a mediator —the money would be restored—and then he, Clifford, would only have to do what the rest of the world were mostly doing, work, and gain an income honorably in some way—probably by means of his brush. Or, should Marsden really have a heart, and any sort of sense of honor, he might—it was just possible—hand over to him out of his abundance, what he must know and feel was justly Clifford's due. Such were his thoughts and hopes, as he lay tossing and turning all that night upon his sleepless bed.

At length came the dawn of the looked-for happy day, and he could lie there no longer, but got up. First he took his usual plunge over the side— which refreshed him and brought the color into his careworn face—and then he dressed himself with more than usual pains, and went ashore. He walked straight to the Hotel, and found the servants already on the move—for in Summer, in that hot climate, the early morning is the pleasantest time, and very early rising is the universal rule. He was shown into the Salon, by the waiter whom he had spoken to on the previous day; and he begged the man to knock at the doors of his friends' rooms, and say that

Mr. Clifford was below,—never for a moment doubting that they would both very soon come down, and greet him with the same kindness as of old,—for if they had not intended this why had they travelled so many hundred miles to see him? Never doubting therefore, but full of impatient hope, he paced the room incessantly, listening to every sound, and with his eyes rivetted upon the door, expecting every moment that it would open, and his long-lost Kate be the first to enter, and rush into his arms.

At length the handle turned, the waiter entered, and put into his hand a parcel from Mr. Bell.

He tore open the wrapper with trembling hands, and found within it the book of his narrative returned, and a letter from his friend. But on the back of the envelope, close above the seal, were written these ominous words: "I trust to your honor to leave us now, and not to open this letter until you are on board the yacht."

His heart began to sink. He burned to open the letter then and there, but his honor was on its trial, and he dared not. He therefore left the house, and hurried at his swiftest pace to the Quay. Happily the dingey was then alongside, and Jim about to go on board in it, with a can of fresh water which he had fetched from a fountain near. At last Clifford was in his cabin; and there, with eager haste, he tore the letter open, and read what follows :—

Clifford, your story is a most painful disappointment to me! I feared it might be, but still I hoped that it might not. Had my faith in you been borne out by that narrative, you would have found that I had made a toilsome and expensive journey in order to save you a few days' delay in hearing of the happiness which might then have been *ours*.

But alas! that cannot be now. You have been guilty of a crime which no man of honor under *any* circumstances could possibly commit, because, as I told you yesterday, he could never consent to be a traitor to the civilization from which he reaps all those blessings that make life dear. No reasoning will justify your crime. It must remain a stigma upon your life; and you ought not to dream of any pure-minded woman sharing your disgrace.

Believe me I am still your friend—your most faithful and devoted friend—but I cannot be *more* than this. No other relation between us can be possible now. I cannot tell you how strongly I feel this—but so it is.

And now I request that, as an atonement for the past, you will help me to soften the affliction to poor Kate. . We shall have left Vigo by the time you have read these lines. I implore you not to follow us. My mind is fully made up as to the course of conduct which I ought to pursue, and I have prayed most earnestly for God's help to go through with it, and do my duty to my child. Time—but above all, *occupation*—will bring relief to *you*. Do not act meanly. Those who once loved you will watch your future career in life with deep interest. Strive to make that such as to prove that you were not altogether unworthy of their regard.

Believe me to remain, ever your most sincere friend, in the very highest meaning of that word,

ALFRED BELL.

Clifford, after reading the above but once, pressed his hands against his throbbing temples— thought intensely for a minute—then took his writing case, and hastily penned the following lines :—

Kate—my best beloved—my only beloved—my dearest, dearest Kate—think of me to-night at sunset, and pray for me *then*. Cherish my memory afterwards. Think sometimes of our past happiness. If my spirit should be permitted to revisit you on earth it will be ever at your side.

Farewell, farewell, farewell, until we meet again in another, and I still hope a happier world!

He wrote these lines through eyes blinded

with tears—he folded them hastily—then rushed on deck, sprang into the dingey, and pulled himself ashore with the energy of a madman. Then he rushed along the streets to that in which was the hotel. A carriage had just left its door, and was being driven swiftly towards him. As it passed, he saw Kate and Mr. Bell inside. The face of the former was buried in her handkerchief, and she was sobbing violently. He rushed up to the carriage door, sprang upon a step, and putting his arm in through the open window, thrust his note between her fingers, and then sprang back again to the ground. The act occupied but a second, and was done with the speed of thought. The carriage did not stop. He staggered towards a wall, against which he leant, and there watched the vehicle roll on. In another minute it had turned a corner of the street, and he could see it no more !

Happily he was alone, or the expression of his face at that moment would have terrified a passer by. We know of nothing in nature to which the outward expression of such anguish as he then felt can be justly compared. The face of a poor horse undergoing vivisection at the hands of a French Medical student would merely express acute physical pain; but there is assuredly in mental agony something far worse than this. Human nature may have to endure worse torture than a lower animal can ever feel. To the sublime pathos of deep *mental* suffering there is nothing in lower nature which can be compared. It stands alone—just as in the physical world do the lightning, the thunder, the earthquake, the tempest-tossed ocean, the avalanche, the flaming comet, the dismal solar eclipse!

Clifford had staked his all of earthly happiness upon his love for Kate, and he had lost his stake. There was nothing more worth living for. A few more hours remained of work below, in which to settle his affairs for the sake of others; and then, with the setting sun, would come—release!

CHAPTER 24.

—

CHRISTIAN MORALS.

CLIFFORD's first paroxysm of grief did not, to all appearance, last long. The sound of the carriage wheels had scarcely ceased before he roused himself, stood erect, and composed his features. Then he walked a few steps—each one being firmer than its predecessor—and then he became *apparently* himself again. This control over the outward expression of suffering is peculiar to the human species. Animals can be patient under physical pain, but their patience is a negative virtue. They never exhibit that pride which *scorns* the expression of pain.

Clifford walked to the corner where the carriage had turned off, in order to see whether it had been detained by any circumstance in the next street; but not seeing it he retraced his steps, and walked at his usual pace towards the hotel, and then past it. He met several people by the way, but none of them remarked anything peculiar in his manner or appearance. He entered a chemist's shop. A chubby little child ran up to him. He patted its cheek and smiled. Then he endeavoured to make the man behind the counter understand the nature of the articles which he wished to purchase. That little difficulty gave rise to some amusing attempts at practically illustrating his wants. One of these articles was a tooth brush, another a cake of soap, a third a box of cough lozenges, a fourth one of those dangerous substances used in medicine, which kill if taken in too large a dose, but of which he required no more than a doctor would prescribe for one dose. After this, he went to three other chemist's shops, and bought similar articles, but always as much of that particular drug as he could obtain without suspicion. In every shop his manner was cheerful, if not absolutely gay. The people who served him thought him a pleasant gentleman. Lastly he strolled to the promenade, and seated himself on his usual bench, which overlooked the roadstead. Happening to have a pocket telescope with him, he put it occasionally to his eye. He also once took out a note book, and set down memoranda of some letters which he wished to write that day.

It was then about eight o'clock in the morning, and it therefore wanted twelve hours to sunset—at which time he had requested Kate to think of him, and to pray for him.

There was no one else on the promenade then, for the place was usually deserted during the day.

He sat for half-an-hour in profound thought, and nearly motionless.

At length he took from his pocket the little parcels of things which he had bought at the three chemists' shops, and spread them on his knee. They consisted of three tooth brushes, a small tooth comb, two boxes of cough lozenges, one of rhubarb pills, a cake of soap, a pot of scented mutton suet, yclept "beard beautifier," some genuine bears'-grease for promoting the growth of the hair, with a portrait of bruin on the lid, some pipe liquorice, and three little paper parcels containing that particular drug, in powder, which was to send the spirit to another if not a happier world.

He opened one of those little parcels—examined its contents both by touch, taste, and smell—smiled—and scattered the powder on the ground. He did the same to the contents of the other two parcels. Just as he had finished, a merry burst of laughter arose from some children who were at play in a garden on the opposite side of a high stone wall, at a few yards distance from him. He got up, went to it, and threw over it amongst the children the articles which had been spread out upon his knee. Presently he heard them laughing again, and scrambling for the things in great glee; and in a minute or two one of the youngsters mounted the wall, and peeped over at him. He had not thrown the galleypot of grease from the haunches of the fine bear which had just been slaughtered, for fear it might strike one of the children on the head; so he handed that up to the youngster in question, who immediately stuck his finger into the contents, and then sucked it, with a wry face. Clifford positively burst out laughing. He then returned to his seat.

After sitting a few minutes in precisely the same posture as before, he got up and took two or three turns on the promenade. He seemed to have grown taller all of a sudden; and although he was not himself conscious of it, his step was proud, stately, and defiant. If Kate had seen him then she would have thought he had never before looked so handsome.

Once more he returned to his seat, put the telescope to his eye, and was watching some operations of Jim's which were going on on board his yacht,—when he felt a light tap upon his shoulder. He turned, and beheld Mr. Bell.

"You see I have come back again already," said that gentleman, offering Clifford his hand.

The latter took it, but not very cordially, and replied quite calmly

"I suppose my note frightened you, Sir. I was very foolish to write it. I ought to have known better. I am sorry you attached any importance to it."

"Well—I confess it has brought me back again—for I know your violent and impulsive temper," said Mr. Bell.

"I must say you have not been addicted to flattering me of late," replied Clifford. "Perhaps some day you may think better of me. That note meant nothing whatever. You should have regarded it as no more than the first moan of a patient, when the surgeon draws his knife across a mass of diseased and swollen flesh. The operator who becomes nervous at that moan is not fit to handle the knife. I fear, Sir, you are but a bungler in your present character of operating surgeon."

" I am truly glad to hear you say so," replied Mr. Bell, "although your remark shows contempt for my own skill."

" You might have known, I think," added Clifford, "that that note was written in a moment of great excitement, and could not possibly mean anything serious. I hardly remember what I said, but I am sure it would raise a smile if we had it now before us."

" Here it is," said Mr. Bell, handing him the note which he had thrust into Kate's hand an hour before.

Clifford read it; then tore it up, and scattered the fragments on the ground—adding

" I hope you did not let your daughter see it."

" I am sorry to say I did; and it created a terrible scene between us—in the midst of which she fainted."

"I am grieved to hear that. Poor Kate! She ought to have known me better. Those lines were merely some melodramatic nonsense which I suppose I must have picked up from a French novel. A brave man can never long contemplate such an act of cowardice as those lines insinuated; and I trust that neither you nor she could suppose me guilty of *that* meanness."

"Then you intend to be a brave good fellow, Clifford, and do battle with your feelings, and conquer them, eh? Is that what you will commission me to tell her?" asked Mr. Bell.

"I was looking at my poor faithful Jim, when you touched me on the shoulder," he replied evasively. "When I left him at five o'clock this morning, to go to see you at the hotel—full of hope then—I told him there might be three of us to breakfast; so I see that he has been borrowing a sail from an English collier in the roads, and is trying to spread it out for an awning. The poor fellow will be sadly cut up when I return alone, and tell him that we are to start to-night, without his old passengers."

There was a pause for a minute or two in

their conversation. When Mr. Bell spoke again his voice betrayed evident emotion.

"Shall you leave so soon?" he asked.

But Clifford made no direct reply. At length he said

"I was trying, as I sat here, to understand the motives of your conduct, and see whether I could reconcile them with humanity."

"Are they not plain enough?" replied Mr. Bell. "Am I not consulting my daughter's happiness, and sacrificing all my own feelings to a strong and manifest sense of duty?"

"Stop; let *me* put the case," said Clifford. "It seems to stand thus: You are a clergyman —a gentleman—a man of respectability—and you do not wish your daughter to ally herself with one who has committed a forgery, and who may at any moment be charged with it, be found guilty, and be transported for life."

"Exactly so. Change places with me, in imagination, for one moment, and you will then perceive that I am right. I should have the opinion of the whole world to back me, if it were put to the vote."

"Then we understand each other," replied Clifford. "Let that pass. Let us change the subject. There are some questions I wish to ask you about Marsden, and his little daughter. You left this morning without giving me the slightest information on points of such vital importance to me to know. On what principle do you defend so unfeeling an act of forgetfulness ? "

To this accusation Mr. Bell replied

"I have written an account of all that occurred that afternoon after you started, and had left it for you at the hotel; but since I came back I called for it, and it is now in my pocket. Take it and read it ; you will find therein all the information you require."

So saying he gave him the manuscript. Clifford took it, and went to read it alone on another seat, at the further end of the promenade. His perusal of it occupied several minutes, although the matter was condensed into a sheet of note paper ; for in his excited state of mind he had to read it over many times before he could clearly comprehend its meaning. And yet it was simple enough, and consisted only of the following terse sentences :—

Marsden is dead ! He was killed in a scuffle with one of the gendarmes, who was arresting him for having broken the law by firing upon you.' No friend_s claimed the body. No articles of any importance were found on his person. He was buried in the cemetery of the gaol at St. Servan. He had charged you with having stolen his yacht, and it was on that charge that your arrest was attempted.

I was standing at the little quay abreast of where the yacht was lying, with Mabel and the *bonne* by my side, waiting for you and Kate to join me, in order that we might all be put on board together by Jim in the dingey, when I heard a heavy plunge in the water not many yards from where I was standing, and presently saw you rise to the surface and swim towards the yacht; after which I heard shots fired at you, and shouting from above. Then I saw Jim put off for you, and save you in the dingey; after which I hastened to the assistance of Kate, who had been left on the platform above. Before I could reach her, however, the fatal scuffle had taken place between the gendarme and Marsden, and I met the two soldiers carrying his dead body along the path! They described minutely all that had occurred.

I reached Kate's side shortly after the yacht had passed out of sight. I then repaired with her, Mabel, and the *bonne*, to the village where we landed, and engaged a boat to take us to St. Malo at once. Your letter was put into my hand by the pilot that night.

Mabel is now with my family in Jersey, who will take care of her until my return. I shall then, of course, await your instructions respecting her.

When Clifford did at length comprehend from the above, that the hated Marsden was really dead, and that he was himself released from the eternal persecution of an implacable foe, earth seemed to become a heaven again, and he could scarcely express an outburst of thankfulness and joy. But then the thought occurred to him that although Mr. Bell was himself aware of the fact, he had nevertheless cancelled his daughter's engagement. Why was that? The answer was evident. Since there were no longer any *material* obstacles in the way of that engagement, the objections to it on Mr. Bell's part must now be entirely *sentimental* ones. At this obvious conclusion Clifford felt deeply hurt; and when he at length reseated himself by the side of his quondam friend, it was without the slightest change in his manner. He was still no more than coldly polite.

"Are you not astonished, and I had almost said delighted, with the information which that paper conveys?" asked Mr. Bell.

"Of course; but now I am all at sea again respecting the motives of your present conduct. I could understand that so long as I was tho object of constant pursuit and revenge by that bad and implacable man, you had good grounds for not allowing your daughter to share my fate. But now, when earth smiles upon me again, what becomes of your objection? Please to state it clearly; and I will then tell you candidly whether I shall respect it as valid, or not."

"My poor fellow," replied Mr. Bell, "if you cannot now understand the impropriety of my permitting an engagement between yourself and my daughter, I shall believe there must still be some obliquity in your moral perceptions. Remember, I have a wife and two other daughters to satisfy as well as myself; and I have a position in society to maintain as a clergyman—who is supposed to set an example in such matters. What would my family, my friends, the world at large think of me, were I to sanction Kate's engagement with a man who for two years had lived in Jersey under a feigned name—who had proclaimed himself falsely to be the father of a certain little girl—who had acted a lie with respect to himself in every important particular for the time I name—and who had once committed a forgery?

Under such circumstances, is it possible that I can sanction your engagement with Kate? You will remember that when I did so before, it was conditional—for I believed you when you intimated that you had done nothing morally wrong. Unfortunately, however, your own account of yourself proves the contrary."

"I thank you, Sir, for putting the matter thus plainly," replied Clifford, "and you must permit me to reply to your remarks with equal candour.

"Now what did my crime, as you call it, really amount to? An error of judgment only, committed under very trying circumstances, and with no friend near to give me advice. My intentions were perfectly honorable, and there was no idea of defrauding or injuring anyone—for I supposed Marsden to be dead. If ever a mistake—for I will *not* call it a crime—was committed under extenuating circumstances, it was mine. But if that disqualifies me, as you say it does, from ever forming an alliance with a pure-minded woman, observe what results. I must either remain single, or else marry a woman of low tastes and low moral tone. Now surely this involves a *reductio ad absurdum*—does it not?

2 Q

"Then again, if none but a faultless being will satisfy you, where is such to be found? Run your eye over the catalogue of great and good men in history, and name one, if you can, who would satisfy your conditions. Do not think me trifling with sacred things if I call to your memory the names of David, Peter, and Paul. The very frailties of human nature seem to me to add another bond of tenderness to friendship and to love. Then, my crime, such as it was, was committed under the firm belief of Marsden's death; but as soon as I found that he was alive, I offered to make full restitution of property, which nevertheless I knew by strict right belonged to myself. Now, under all these circumstances, I call on you to ask yourself whether you are acting on broad Christian principles, or merely according to conventional notions of *taste* and *propriety*, in cancelling my engagement with Kate?"

"On *both* principles," was Mr. Bell's reply, "for the two are, or ought to be, in harmony with each other."

"Then I fear," replied Clifford, "that our ideas are widely different. Your moral code is too sentimental and theoretical for me. It ignores altogether a great fact in nature. It is unpractical, and consists of mere words, and lectures, and questions of taste and etiquette. It is the moral code of a man who has lived in a favoured position above the arena in which the struggle of human life goes on. It is the very code which the Saviour condemned. There is no heart, no large human sympathy in it. It is cold, calculating, unfeeling. By it the sinner, however penitent, is debarred from grace. I have been grievously mistaken in you. Your profession of friendship is a mere empty word. My real friend now is a poor sinner like myself, a man in humble station, in a rough sailors' garb, with tarry hands and uncombed locks. When I go on board and tell that man my sad story, depend upon it he will condemn you,—for he is one of the toilers of the world, and his instincts, which were right by nature, have been kept right by use. Jim will condemn you; and so will your daughter Ellen; and so, I am certain, does my poor Kate, whose happiness you would sacrifice to an idea—a point of propriety—a question of taste. If you persist in your present conduct you will have a cold and unfeeling heart; and bitter as the trial may be to Kate to oppose your wishes in this matter, I shall use all my influence to persuade her to do so. This morning I yielded passive obedience to a decree which seemed right at the time, and against which my pride forbad me to expostulate,—for how could I entreat you to reverse it and allow your daughter to share the fate of an outcast, against your own moral convictions and apparently hers also? But now that I have heard of Marsden's death, the case becomes widely different. I have ceased to be an outcast. I can enter into society again without fear, and safe from persecution. The sword which during his lifetime might have constantly hung over me has fallen harmless, and I am free. Therefore I say now, cancel your letter to me—retract your refusal to my engagement with Kate—or I declare open war with you at once. What have you to say to this?"

Mr. Bell did not immediately reply. He was evidently much agitated, but his countenance betrayed no sign of anger at Clifford's somewhat strong and rude remarks. He was by nature an extremely kind-hearted and good-tempered man, besides which the control of temper had become habitual to him, and a matter of principle which he always strove to obey. But he did not even *feel* angry. His agitation proceeded from a struggle between his affections and what he had at first considered to be his duty in opposition to them. At length he said, in the very kindest tone

" Clifford, don't misunderstand me. My heart pleads for you. You need no advocate there. Much of what you say is right and good; but remember how young Kate is—how short a time you have known her—how slight after all the impression may be that you have really made upon her. If she were five years older, and you had known her by just so much longer; and if what may now be only a romantic feeling should actually have taken such deep root as to affect seriously the happiness of both your lives, then I might take a very different view of the matter. It is because I hardly believe that either her feelings or yours can have become too deeply interested, that I have desired, under the changed aspect of your circumstances, to nip this attachment in the bud. You see I am not so heartless as you think. I am willing to make a rational concession to what you call broad Christian principles, and to admit the universality of human frailty as well as the efficacy of repentance. If you are both so deeply attached as to render the cancelling of your engagement a blow which would absolutely embitter the whole of your future lives, then—then—"

"Then," said Clifford, interrupting him, and with a returning smile, "Then you will allow the matter to turn upon whether Kate really loves me or not, after a sufficient term of probation? So be it. I accept these conditions; and I would suggest to you as the best means of making your experiment, that you both return with me to Jersey in the yacht. You owe me this for having been my passenger at all, and for having thrown us so much together, and encouraged my suit. I cast myself upon your generosity. I will answer for the state of my own affections. The happiness of my own life, at any rate, is at stake. Two months ago possibly your objections might have been valid, but they are not so now. Prove to us both that you have a heart."

Mr. Bell heaved a deep sigh, and replied

" You are all wrong, Clifford, and I know it, and could prove it to you if I had *not* a heart—but—but—oh dear ! What will they say to me at home ? How ever shall we get out of the scrape ? "

" Now, dear Sir," said Clifford, " you are not acting—you are yourself again. What has happened during the last few hours has been a hideous mistake—an attempt of yours to solve a pure problem of feeling without the intervention of the heart. May I offer you my hand once more, and ask you to forgive the past, and think as kindly of me as you once did ? "

The old clergyman took his young friend's hand, and pressed it warmly.

" Clifford," he said, " I loved you, and it is I who have really suffered most from all this horror. But it is over now. I yield the point. I am helpless. Two young hearts have proved more than a match for an old man's scruples. Kate's entreaties almost prevailed against them last night, and now your remonstrances have left me helpless. There — go now—and leave me to myself to make peace as best I may with my own conscience. I will join you by-and-bye on board the yacht."

CHAPTER 25.

—

AN ENGLISH GIRL IN A SPANISH BOWER.

CLIFFORD did as he was told with the greatest alacrity; that is to say, he left his old friend on the promenade to his own meditations, and went his way. Where that way led him the reader will easily guess—to the hotel where Kate was staying. He seemed to walk on air, and the distance to it from the promenade appeared to have dwindled to a fourth of what it was—or rather to no distance at all if measured by time. When he got there he asked no one's leave, and made no more enquiries of the cautious English waiter, but mounted at once to Kate's room, and tapped at the door.

No one answered. She was not within. What

had become of her? He must find the English waiter after all and enquire.

The latter came to his assistance, and informed him that the young lady was then in a summer house, or belvedere, upon the roof of the building, which commanded a view of the Harbour. He piloted him to the foot of some stairs which led to the same, and Clifford strode up them three at a time. At the top of all there was a door which opened upon a lead flat; and then, opposite to him was the building in question. The door was shut. He tapped, and Kate opened it. She had been sitting there alone, looking through a glass at the shipping in the roads—or rather at a particular ship—the dear little BAGATELLE, with her British ensign and Irish burgee.

Clifford stood before her, with joy and hope beaming in every feature. A single glance at his happy face was enough. There was no resisting it—no time then for buts, and ifs, and questionings. She put her two hands upon his broad shoulders—they gazed fondly into each other's eyes for an instant—and then he pressed her to his heart once more.

We will not repeat their first expressions

of delight at meeting, after those anxious days and recent hours of trouble; but by means of her lover's first broken sentences Kate understood that he had seen her Papa—had had a long talk with him—that he had " come round"—and that it was " all right now."

" And what do you think, my Kate," he added, as soon as he could collect ideas enough for an entire sentence—" What do you think is the only difficulty in our way now? Your Papa is not satisfied that we love each other enough. His fear is that we have only formed a romantic attachment which could easily be nipped in the bud. It all turns now on whether we love each other enough. That is what he doubts, and what we have got to prove to him. So you are to go back with me in the yacht, just by way of an experiment as to the intensity of our affection. Isn't it ecstatic, after all this morning's horrid work ?"

" Dear, kind old Papa!" said Kate. " I know that it would come to this at last. You can't imagine what an affectionate creature he is. Our carriage this morning was only engaged for one stage, and I am sure he was quite glad of any excuse to turn back. But,

you very naughty one, you don't know how
you frightened me by that note ; and Papa too,
for he said he knew your violent temper."

" But Katie, only think what a poor wretch
I was then. *You* lost to me—the hope I had
of your Father's mediation with Marsden cut
off—the hand of every man against me—only
fancy what *that* means—and to lead the life
of a flying fish, hunted eternally, and never at
peace day or night ! And then, if caught at last,
to be tried for a felon's crime, and condemned
to pay the horrible penalty for the rest of my
life ! Fancy, if you can, the loss of liberty
for ever—the prison dress—the lash for every
slight offence—the hair cropped close—the
odious profitless toil—the mind snuffed out—
the dreary, weary, hopeless future ! Such, at
least, in that paroxysm was the picture presented
by my disordered brain. If then, in my despair,
I did meditate for a brief half hour such an
act as my note insinuated, there was some
excuse. But it was not in my nature that
such a thought should continue long. The
fit soon wore off. I was in my right senses
again when your father found me."

" My poor —— What name must I call you

now?" she asked, looking with amusing *naïveté* into his face.

" Your poor Harry, if you like. Don't you like Henry Clifford better than John Smith?"

She smiled at this question, but evaded a direct reply by answering

" But what a strange story your's was! I read it last night. Do you know I always felt certain there was something mysterious about you? I have seen you sometimes not answer to your old name; and I was quite sure that Mabel was not your daughter. You liked her — you loved her even — but it was not a *father's* love—it was an elder brother's rather."

" Then you knew all along what I dared not tell you—that *you* were really my first, first love—and you believed in me in spite of my mysteriousness?"

" Women have instincts in such matters, and I suppose these are always right. But what a deal we have got to talk about. And your poor shoulder—how is that now? I see it is still bandaged up."

" A mere trifle—but it throbs sometimes. It throbbed last night when I stood before you in the street. Why wouldn't you speak to a poor fellow at first, Katie? It seemed so cruel of you."

" Because Papa had made me promise I would not, only five minutes before. I had just finished reading your narrative, and he came in and told me that it was to be all over between us, and that I was never to speak to you again—never—never!"

" And you promised you would not?"

" I thought it best to do so, for I knew he would come round in time."

" But what a journey you must have had—all through the heat and dust from St. Malo!"

" No, it was a delicious journey. We crossed the Pyrenees. Oh, such lovely scenery; and we were both in such high spirits all the way at the thoughts of taking you by surprise. That was why Papa did not write. The misery only began last night. Papa never dreamt of your having done anything really wrong—only something very foolish, perhaps— or rash."

" So you enjoyed crossing the mountains," replied Clifford, evasively. " They were a new idea—a real treat—were they not?"

" And the sunrises we saw—oh, how grand they were amongst the mountain passes !

" And the sunsets too?" enquired Clifford. " And then you thought of the Grand Bey? I almost think you did?"

" Ah yes!—and our strange presentiments !" she added, smiling.

" Tell me where you slept at St. Malo that night after the yacht left," enquired Clifford.

" At the Hotel de France. I had a little upper room overlooking the sea. I sat at the window for hours that night, thinking of you two poor things all alone in the yacht—and it seemed to blow so—and the sea looked so wild—and I saw the sunset *that* night too."

" And did you bestow one little tear on the memory of the poor wanderer ? Tell me—I almost think you did."

" Just one perhaps—and then I sat at my table, and made that little sketch I sent you. Did you understand it? I dared not write you a line, because I had promised Papa I would not. But after all, what could a whole quire of words have told you more than *hope?*"

" And so your Papa came here, quite intend-ing to go back with me in the yacht? I

never could have dreamt that from his manner.
You can't think how cold he was at first."

"I knew him better—and so will you some
day. He is such a dear kind creature—and
we all love him so at home. If anything goes
wrong he reasons with us, and reasons, and
reasons, and then at last he makes it up. But
you must know we never have any secrets
from him—for that's a thing he can't forgive.
But don't let us talk about this now. Tell
me what that dear old Jim is doing in the
yacht. I've been watching him for the last
hour. He has been spreading an awning over
the deck, and sprinkling it with water, and
bringing up a table, and laying a cloth, and
putting things out, I suppose for breakfast
in the open air. It seems all ready now; and
he is waiting for some one in the dingey at
the water side."

"He is waiting for *us*, my child," said her
Father, smiling, and putting his hands upon
her shoulders from behind. He had stolen upon
them unperceived, and had heard every syllable
that his Kate had said about him.

"Oh Papa, how you made me jump!" she
said, looking timidly into his face.

He stroked her soft waving tresses affection-
ately, and patted her pale cheek—for it was
pale that morning—and said in a whisper

" Run, Kate, and put your bonnet on, or Jim's
patience will be worn out."

She threw her arms round her Papa's neck, and
kissed him fondly ; then ran off to her own room.

Clifford watched her till she was out of sight,
and thought she had never looked half so beautiful, and that he had never loved her half so
well as he did then.

" My poor fellow," said Mr. Bell to him as
soon as they were alone, " forgive me if I
have caused you pain to-day. I am afraid
you thought me a most unpleasant old bore,
and an ungrateful one too for all your kindness."

" Well really, my dear Sir, if you will have
the plain truth," said Clifford, smiling, " you
did contrive to make yourself, for about three
hours, as intensely disagreeable as a man well
could in that limited time."

" I may ask you perhaps to sign a certificate
to that effect, when we get home," said Mr. Bell.

" But if I do," replied Clifford, " you must
endorse it with your solemn promise never to
behave thus again."

"We shall see." replied his old friend. "But let us go on board now. I don't feel at home here a bit; and we have got a world of things to talk about yet. Poor Katie wants rest too, —and she will be glad, I know, to stretch herself again upon her old berth.

They had not long to wait for her; and in another ten minutes the trio were once more on board the BAGATELLE.

CHAPTER 26.

AT SEA AGAIN.

" Well Jim," said Mr. Bell, as he crept under the awning, out of the broiling sunshine, and looked at the good things which the said Jim had been spreading out for breakfast—including fish and fruit from the early Market, " Well Jim—here we are, back again at last."

" In course you are, your honor," replied the good fellow addressed, with a broad grin. " I know'd you wouldn't be long away—and I told our young cap'n so, lots of times. Not as I know much about you gen'l'folks either, —but I could see pretty plain as how you liked him, and I said to him many times, when he was well nigh giving in, don't take on like that, my lad—just give 'em a fortnight or so more, and they'll turn up again—you see.

They ain't a-going to leave you in the lurch. And as to what you've been and done years ago—why that ain't nothing, I know—and the old gen'l'man will put that straight with the big wigs over the water—and then it'll be all plain sailing again, and stun-s'ls set alow and aloft."

"I don't know, Jim, about that," replied Mr. Bell, smiling. "I'm afraid you sadly overrate my influence with your supposed big-wigs. Don't you know that I am only a poor parson, living in a little quiet country village, out of the great world?"

Jim grinned, as much as to insinuate that he knew better; and added

"Well—it's a good job you've all come back anyhow—for when I seed him cut off this morning in the dingey, and run like a mad dog along the Pier, I said to myself—clap a stopper on that, somebody—and take a turn."

"But you set to work, Jim, and got the breakfast ready, nevertheless."

"In course I did. I know'd the first sight of the young lassie would bring him up sharp. Gen'l'folks are like the rest on us, for that. We're all spun out of the same yarns—only one's rope's hawser-laid, and another's served and wormed, and another's only a plain twist."

The above elegant conversation was confined to themselves,—for Kate had dived down the companion, and Clifford was awaiting her return, with curiosity at the result.

She soon came back and asked him, with a smile, for the key of the ladies' cabin, as the door was locked.

He took it from a safe corner of his coat pocket, where it had remained ever since the afternoon when he and Jim left St. Malo together, and gave it her.

In a few minutes she returned again.

" Well," he asked, " did you find your things all right?"

" Yes—exactly as we left them—not a thing touched—Mabel's box of soldiers, and the *bonne's* cap, and the book of sketches half open, just as I left it when we started for our walk."

" Katie—do you know what vow I made that day, when I locked the door?"

" No—what?"

" That no one should ever open it again until your little fingers turned the key."

" You silly creature! "

"Come, Kate, my child," cried her father, from the breakfast table. "We are all ready and waiting—you forget we've had no breakfast yet—and it's near eleven o'clock."

There is nothing romantic in unalloyed happiness; that may always be left to the imagination of the reader; so a very few words will suffice for a detail of the principal events of the next few days.

The yachting party remained nearly a week longer at Vigo, in order to see the place and take some trips in the vicinity; and then they started for Jersey. Jim found a young English sailor to share the forecastle with him, and bear a hand; and the waiter at the hotel recommended a French girl, to attend upon Kate. But if the truth must be told, Mr. Bell did not look forward without misgivings to crossing the dreaded Bay, and being perhaps a week at sea in a craft of only eight and twenty tons, N.M.—to say nothing of the chances there were of the heavy contributions which old Neptune might exact by the way. Kate, however, was in high spirits, and laughed at such chances, and to her the idea of the trip home was all *couleur de rose.* Fancy, how much she would have to tell her Mamma and sisters when she got back—all about the Pyrenees, and the coast of Spain, and—the reader can guess what else. There was only one thing which they all regretted, and that was the absence of little Mabel. Children are troublesome, it is true ; but how one misses their merry prattle and funny ways when they are not rollicking about. What a sober old world it is then.

On their first stroll together in the promenade Kate gave Clifford a present which she had brought for him from St. Malo, and the cost of which had nearly run away with all her pocket money—for she had bought it unknown to her good Papa. What does the reader suppose it was ? A new sketching-block exactly like the first—and the very thing he wanted. What tact the women have in all these matters —have they not ? How sure they are, when they make you a present, to give you the very thing you most want.

So Clifford took some souvenirs of Vigo, without delay ; and you may be sure that the old bench on the promenade—the view from thence over the roadstead, with the BAGATELLE at anchor—the garden wall over which he had thrown the things to the children—and the window of the hotel at which he had seen Kate, were amongst them. He added also a few comic pages and sketches to her diary of the trip.

It was a fine afternoon in August, just a week after they had left Vigo. A six-knot breeze from the nor'west was ruffling the green sea with little dancing waves, and the BAGATELLE was bowling along before it, with both her jib-headed topsails and her squaresail set. Jersey could be seen like a long thin grey line upon the horizon; and behind them were the Roches Douvres, so graphically described in Victor Hugo's "Toilers of the Sea." Their trip was now really drawing to a close; and they talked of anchoring in the small roads of St. Helier before dusk that night. Jim was at the helm—his pal was chatting with him at his side—the French girl was getting tea ready below—Kate was seated on a buffet stuffed with cork, in the shadow of the mainsail, watching the bubbles as they danced merrily by, and indulging in her own sweet fancies whatever those might be—and Mr. Bell and Clifford were together for'ard, looking out a-head, and sitting with their backs against the windlass, chatting, and the latter solacing himself at the same time with a cheroot.

" I am not by any means sure," said Mr. Bell, " that you will be quite safe in Jersey yet. Suppose Marsden should have kept the original will, and have left it with the old man at La Pulente. He seems to be an unprincipled scamp, that; and he might take advantage of you if he could turn a penny by so doing. Or suppose Marsden should have had a friend to whom he communicated the circumstances of the case, and who might take it up with the hope of extorting money from you, as a bribe to keep silent respecting what he knew. The affair has still a threatening look, I think."

" I don't agree with you quite," said Clifford, in reply. "The old man is not altogether bad. He is a character in his way, and I have made rather a study of him for the last two years. There is good in him; and his meanness is not natural—it is an acquired vice. I believe he would rather serve me than a stranger—

even if the balance did preponderate a little in favour of my foe."

"You know best, of course — but it won't do to trust him too far. I confess I am getting nervous as I get near home."

"And beginning to repent, perhaps," said Clifford, somewhat coldly, "that you did not leave me to my fate."

"Hush!" said Mr. Bell. "You know I have acted for the best, so far as my poor judgment went, for you and Kate, regardless of myself and of what the world may say of me. I had a long, a very long talk with her that night, after she had read your story. I then represented to her the danger in which you might still stand after your return to English soil — the possibility of all sorts of horrors turning up — the all but certainty there was that you would be compelled to live abroad — the remonstrances of my own family and friends against the match — the secrecy and misery which a long engagement might involve — in fact, I entreated her to break it off. I had come to disapprove of it myself when I found what a bad case it was, according to your own confession; and I pointed out to her that my objections were not founded on false sentiment or narrow views, but on common sense, such as every one would approve."

" And what was her reply ? " asked Clifford.

" A woman's—every word," replied Mr. Bell. " She said, the deeper you might be in the mire the more she should love you and cling to you, and the more resolved she should become to share your fate. In fact, she defied her poor old Father. I never saw her so animated. It almost made me smile. It proved to me that she loved you ; and I had then to learn whether you really loved her. The next morning was to afford me the test of that. You remember what occurred, and how you defied me too. Then I saw that both your minds were made up, and that it would be as cruel as useless of me to interfere. I gave way. And now, Clifford, believe me I have nothing to regret. Personally I like you, and I believe in your integrity. You have nothing to fear from any change in me ; and as the rest of my family take their tone from me, you will be favourably received by them also. But we must carefully weigh all the risks and liabilities before you set your foot on shore."

"My own idea was this," replied Clifford. "For me to go to the old man, take him by surprise, and judge for myself how the land lies."

"No, no. Let me go alone first, as your representative," said Mr. Bell. "Then I would make him a definite offer as regards an annuity, in order to place him beyond the reach of temptation; and hear what he would have to say. In the meantime you could remain on board, and be ready to start again in the event of there being any risk of your arrest. The production of the real will, backed by the evidence of the old man as to what Marsden may have communicated to him, might be highly serious. It might involve your forced confession, and an appeal for pardon to the Crown. You must remember that in spite of your conciliatory letter old Smith betrayed you. He may not possibly have heard of Marsden's death since then. Going to see him yourself would be very hazardous, I think."

"I tell you what," said Clifford. "Suppose we go to him together to-night. We could anchor in St. Brelade's Bay, only two miles from the cottage, and the yacht would lie there safe enough, with this wind, until we come back. Look—the cottage is already in sight. I just caught a flash of sun-light reflected from the little window in the gable end. There it is again. We shall be in Jersey in another hour or two. Let us both go and see the old scamp to-night."

So thus it was arranged between them.

We must remind the reader that neither Mr. Bell nor Clifford knew anything then of what had occurred between old Smith and Marsden at their interview, related in a preceding chapter. All they knew was, that notwithstanding Clifford's apologetic letter to Smith, and the offer of the annuity, the latter had betrayed him to his foe.

CHAPTER 27.

A SCENE IN AN ATTIC.

THE moon had just risen above the sand-hills of St. Ouen's that night, when three persons presented themselves at the humble doorway of La Bie cottage, and knocked for admittance. They were Mr. Bell, Clifford, and Kate. The latter had begged so hard of her Papa to be allowed to go too, that he had not been able to refuse her request.

Hannah had already gone to bed; but she dressed herself with haste, and went to the door.

Clifford was the first to speak. He offered his hand to Hannah, and said, as she took it with unfeigned pleasure at seeing him again,

" Can we speak a word or two with your Father to-night? "

" Oh, dear yes—of course you can—he will be delighted to see you—pray come in."

So they were all shown into the parlour on the ground floor, whilst Hannah went up to her Father, to prepare him to receive his visitors.

" I knew Clifford's voice," he whispered, " but who are the other two? "

" An old clergyman and a young lady," was the reply.

" Ah — the same who went with him in the yacht — of course.   Mr. Bell and his daughter. Show up the two gentlemen, Hannah ; the young lady you can entertain yourself, in the room below.

Clifford and Mr. Bell mounted the step ladder, and presented themselves before old Smith.

" You are looking all the better for your voyage," he said to Clifford. " I am glad to see you back."

" Why ? " asked Clifford, laconically.

" Because I like you," was the terse reply.

" Then why did you betray me to Marsden ? "

" I will tell you," said the old man, " if you really don't understand.   I did it on the same principle that I would have killed and eaten you, had I been starving for food. You have heard of boats' crews casting lots, and people eating their best friends; and I dare say you have thought it right—and so it was. The first necessities of life *must* be provided for, at *any* cost. We are animals, and all the rest is secondary, and comes next, when our pressing animal wants have been supplied. If the crew could have caught a fat turtle alongside, they would not have cast lots, and have eaten each other until there was only one left. Is my reasoning suggestive? Does my logic satisfy you? Can you see its application to our own case ?"

"Ask my friend the clergyman what he thinks," replied Clifford. "He knows all the facts."

"May I venture to offer a remark or two?" asked Mr. Bell.

"By all means," said the old man.

"Then I understand your plea to be this,— you were sorely tempted, and you fell."

"Exactly so. The case before me was simply this—to sacrifice my own life, or to betray my friend. I chose the latter course. The animal and the moral pulled different ways, and the animal triumphed. Whether that was right or wrong, no one ought to say whose moral sentiments have never triumphed over his own animal instincts in a similar contest. A crime, and the temptation to it, should never be separated; they should be weighed against each other in opposite scales. The difference determines the true amount of moral turpitude when the wrong scale goes down. You must never judge of a crime in the abstract."

"But forgive me if I remind you," replied Mr. Bell, "that society provides an alternative to meet these cases of over-temptation. There is the workhouse for the destitute."

"True. There was Lambeth workhouse for me. Society could do no more, I grant. But the transporting me from here to the romantic parish in which I was born would have been excruciating. The journey would have killed me by inches. It would have occasioned my death by torture. And who would have cared for the death or the sufferings of a pauper?"

"Let us change the subject," said Clifford. "Did you ever get my letter which I posted to you at St Malo, in reply to your's to me?"

"Do you mean my first letter, which the boatman took; or my second, addressed to you *Poste Restante* St. Malo, in your true name?" asked the old man.

"Your second? I don't understand you. I never had but one—that which the boatman brought me."

"Then you have not received my second letter, containing the news about my interview with Marsden, and what occurred on that occasion—Eh?"

"I have not indeed," replied Clifford.

"And still you come to see me!" said the old man, with a peculiar expression, and a half smile at an idea which occurred to him at the moment. "That was very imprudent, Mr. Clifford. Do you know that you have placed yourself in my power—and that you deserve your fate for your stupidity? Am I a man, think you, to forgive and forget such insults as you have heaped upon me?

"Fate?—Stupidity?" replied Clifford. "I don't know what you mean, Sir. Explain yourself, if you please."

The old man's reply was given with singular slowness and distinctness, and as he spoke he fixed his eyes upon Clifford's, and watched intently the effect of his communication. He said

"You had no right to count on my forbearance. You had no right to assume that I should forgive your insulting message sent to me by the boatman. You might have known that I should at once write to England on the receipt of such a message, without waiting for any further communication from you. You might have known that your penitent letter would arrive too late to prevent my betraying you. And so it really happened. Now listen. I am in the interest of your foe'; and he has put his case into the hands of the authorities here. I saw the yacht approach the island three hours ago. I immediately sent word of it to the town. She has no doubt been seized by this time; and a party of police have already tracked your footsteps hither. I heard them a minute ago outside the cottage, whilst your friend was suggesting that I should go to the workhouse. In five minutes you will be their prisoner. Your liberty will be gone for ever. A something worse than the honest man's workhouse awaits yourself; and you will not have your friend there to comfort you with his moral reflections on your fall."

At that moment a knock was heard at the door below, and a man's gruff voice without called on Hannah peremptorily to open it, and let him in. What old Smith had said about the police appeared to be only too true!

Clifford cast a hasty glance around the room. The little window was just large enough for his body to pass through, but he would be cut to pieces by the strong fragments of the plate glass. To rush down stairs would have been to leap into the very arms of the police. To spring up to the roof—dash off some tiles —and force himself between the rafters, which were rather wide apart, seemed his only chance. He was about to make this desperate attempt to escape, when the old man called out

"Stop—that won't help you—it is sheer madness. I can save you—but it must be on one condition—the same old story over again. Read this paper, which I have drawn up ready to meet this possible contingency. Sign it, and you shall be free—not a soul shall touch you— a word of mine shall save you."

"What is this?" said Clifford, casting his

eye over the following unsigned document which the old man had put into his hand : —

Jersey, —, —.

One Month after date, I promise to pay to John Smith, or order, One Thousand Pounds, value received.

£1000.

" Never ! " said Clifford. " You should have the last drop of my blood before I would sign that. Old scoundrel ! I defy you and all your arts ! "

" But Clifford—my dear fellow—think," said Mr. Bell, " think of the consequences of your refusal. For Kate's sake—for Mabel's sake— for all our sakes—sign it, I implore you. There is no time to lose."

" And what if I do sign it ? " said Clifford to the old man. " How can you then save me from arrest ? "

" The moments are precious," replied Smith. " There is no time to parley—I can't explain that now—I hear Hannah already at the door."

Mr. Bell put the pen into Clifford's hand, and the old man passed him the ink—but still he hesitated.

" This is rank cowardice and folly," he said.

" Oh, sign it—for pity's sake, sign it," said Mr. Bell.

" I will NOT ! " said Clifford ; and he tore the document to fragments, and flung them on the floor.

A man's heavy footstep was now heard upon the ladder. It was too late for Clifford to attempt an escape by the roof. He turned and faced the door. The lion stood at bay. How many of his adversaries could he upset and leap over, as he made one bound from the top of the step ladder to the passage, and thence out ? Such was his momentary thought.

The door opened, and Jim walked in !

" I thought I 'd just come up arter you," he said, " and keep an eye on the old man—I know'd he 'd be glad to see me."

" What 's all this folly ? " said Clifford. " Are there any other men down below, Jim ? "

" None, as I could see," replied Jim.

" Clifford," said the old man, " May I ask you one last favour ? Let me feel your pulse."

" If you were not a bedridden old fool, I 'd half strangle you," said Clifford ; but at the same time, in a grim vein of comedy, offering him his wrist.

" You are a bold fellow," said Smith, as he felt and counted its regular pulsations; "and you ought to be Admiral of the Channel Fleet. There is no fitful jerking and fluttering that I can hear. The thumps are as steady as a steam-engine at work. And now for your reward —for I have taken a mighty fancy to you. Do you know this document? Take it—it is yours —I obtained possession of it by a stratagem— and I now give it back into the hand of its rightful owner—and I cast myself upon his forgiveness and generosity."

So saying, he placed the original will in Clifford's hand. The story of the police, the unsigned note, &c., had it been no more than a joke? Who can say?

Clifford examined the will for a moment; then folded it up, and put it into his pocket, with the utmost *sangfroid*.

" Did you ever receive my letter, Smith?" he asked, in a more friendly tone. "I mean the one I wrote to you that day on board the BAGATELLE, and posted at St. Malo the same night?"

" I did, and I answered it," was the reply, " but you don't seem to have received my answer. It was addressed to you at St. Malo, *Poste Restante*."

" I have never had it to this day. What were its contents?" enquired Clifford.

" I agreed," said Smith, " to accept the annuity which you offered me as an acknowledgement of services rendered to Mabel. You remember making me that offer, of course? But if not, I have still your letter by me. It was a definite proposition, and one upon which I acted on your behalf."

" Then," said Clifford, " I am now a debtor, by my own showing—so hand me the pen and ink again, and a fresh sheet of paper."

The old man did so; and Clifford wrote a second promissory note, worded as the other had been, but with this exception, that he substituted the name of Hannah for that of John.

" Understand me, Smith," he said, as he handed it to the old man. " I regard this donation, not as the reward of your successful artifice, but as Hannah's reward for saving Mabel's life, and all her subsequent kindness to the child. The money is your daughter's, and not your's. I wish I could say that I like you, and respect you, more than I do."

" But I have still some questions to put to you, Clifford," said the old man.

" I will answer them by letter," was the reply. " I wish you good night."

" Clifford," said Mr. Bell, when they had had all assembled in the lower room, " Your conduct was magnificent, but frightfully risky ! I trembled for you. My heart was in my mouth. It was a happiness that it ended as it did. Jim, I have often been charmed with the sight of your jolly red face, but never so much as I was just now."

" The old man's a crafty one—ain't he, your honor?" said Jim, grinning. "I know'd there'd be a scrimmage when my master got alongside of him—and that's why I came up just to see the fun, and in case I might be wanted."

On their way out, Kate promised Hannah to bring Mabel over one day to see her; and Clifford added

" I have given your Father a thousand pounds for you, Hannah. Mind he doesn't chisel you out of it. It will buy you an annuity, for all your kindness to the child. God bless you. I thank you a thousand times. Good-bye."

They were off before Hannah, in the fulness of her heart, could find words for a reply.

On their way back to the yacht Kate was regaled by her Papa with the full particulars of her lover's magnificent conduct, as he called it, with old Smith, whilst she was in the room below.

They slept on board the yacht that night, as she lay at anchor in the little Boilly roadstead of St. Brelade's Bay; and the next morning they weighed anchor, and took her up to her old quarters with the flood tide. At high water the BAGATELLE was safely moored again in her old berth in St. Helier's Harbour, after an eventful and never-to-be-forgotten trip.

CHAPTER 28.

NEW FRIENDS—THE END.

THE reader must now stride over a few weeks in imagination, while we shift the scene to the quiet little rectory of ———, a village situated amongst the stately trees and undulating slopes of one of the midland counties, and of which Mr. Bell had been for five and twenty years the much respected incumbent.

A part of the flower garden of the parsonage was wisely devoted to a perfectly level and close shaven lawn, not cut up, as was too often the case with lawns before the introduction of the modern game of Croquet, by a number of little flower beds of tadpole and other fantastic shapes, but left clear for playing bowls upon, or lawn billiards, or battledore and shuttlecock, or any similar out-of-door game that everybody finds

amusement in at times. Such was the nice
and useful lawn ; and at one end of it was
an arbour, overhung by trees, with ivy and
honeysuckle creeping over it, and having a
table in the centre and a seat all round—but
not formed of three uncomfortably knotted limbs
of trees, but of nice smooth well-planed planks,
with another to lean your back against ; for
this arbour, be it known, was a little room in
the fresh air, intended for use, and not for
picturesqueness only.

It was one of those calm golden days in the
early part of October, when the equinoxial
gales are past, and the trees have put on
their autumnal livery, and the sun comes out
lazily through the haze at eleven, and pops
in again at two. It was the middle, and the
sunniest part of one of those calm golden days.
Kate and her cousin Annie, a merry clever
spinster of thirty, who has not before been
introduced to the reader, were playing at Les
Graces upon the aforesaid lawn, with sticks and
hoops; Mabel was romping about in her usual
high spirits; Sophy and Ellen were in doors
with their Mamma, very busy indeed, for the
morrow was to be an eventful day in that

little household (can the reader guess why?);
and from the arbour were proceeding both the
smoke and the odour of cigars; while upon
its table still remained the debris of a rather
substantial luncheon, of which its occupants had
just partaken. - These consisted of the good
Rector himself, our friend Henry Clifford, and
a middle-aged gentleman who was the very
personification of fun and good humour, the
father of Cousin Annie aforesaid, and the
younger brother of Mr. Bell, by name "Uncle
Jack."

The three were engaged in such gossip as the
event which was to come off on the following
morning might be supposed to suggest, viz.,
the bridegroom's future prospects—now under
discussion by the same parties for the fiftieth
time.

"My only fear, Jack, is," said Mr. Bell,
" that if you build your river yacht, or barge,
or whatever you like to call it, and take Harry
to Brittany with you, you'll make him as idle
as you are yourself; and that won't do at all,
because his five or six hundred a-year and your
five or six thousand are vastly different things.
You married a fortune; but Kate, poor child,

hasn't got a penny, except the little I can leave her at my death. I want to impress upon him that in all probability he will have to work some day to increase his income, and therefore the sooner he begins the better. What say you, Harry? Am I right or not?"

"Most decidedly you are right," was Clifford's reply. "I have been idle quite long enough, and I mean to buckle to now in earnest, and follow my own profession of landscape painting. The Arts are beginning to be largely encouraged, and will be more so every year as people get wiser and wealthier."

"Well then," said Uncle Jack," it all amounts to what I have been trying to beat into your two noddles for the last month—that my proposed expedition will be the very thing for Harry to join me in. There will be Annie as a companion for Kate—everything as comfortable as in our own homes — Jim to work the boat, a French cook, and a *bonne* to look after Mabel. And then Harry and I will bring out together a book of the trip. I'll do the antiquarian parts, he the illustrations, and the two girls the log and the comicalities between them. The rivers of Brittany are a complete *terra incognita* both to artists and tourists; and what can be more lovely than the scenery of the Vilaine, the Blavet, the Erdre, the Oust, and the Aulne? I have tramped it all, and know it well. And then, by building a suitable barge with six cabins, and living entirely on board, you avoid all the dirt and discomfort of the picturesqueness which you go to see, and it gives you time for writing and sketching on the very spot. We shall be a jolly party; and, in fact, I've set my heart upon it, and the thing is to be."

"Well," said Mr. Bell, "It's as Harry likes. So long as he doesn't settle down into confirmed idleness, without a hobby, reading newspapers, novels and magazines by day, and playing whist at night, and doing nothing that is original with his own faculties, I don't care. Let a man have a hobby, and work at it in earnest, I say; and that will keep his faculties bright, and he will take a practical view of things; but a mere life of reading papers, and gossiping, and criticising, is no intellectual training at all; and a man's taste becomes ignorantly fastidious, and his opinion on any practical question of common sense not worth a dump. Besides which, the chances are that as he grows grey over this sort of work, he becomes mean, selfish, and helpless. When a man with an independence degenerates into the useless kind of being I describe, it is a sin and a shame, and I regard him as one of the blemishes and eyesores of civilized life. Work is a necessity of a healthy state of mind, just as exercise is necessary to bodily health. I am not talking at *you*, Jack, because your antiquarian pursuits *are* a hobby."

Kate and Annie now joined them.

" The barge again, Papa ? " said the latter. " Are you still talking about that everlasting barge, when there is a pretty yacht all ready, and only waiting for us to step on board, at Weymouth ? I am quite of Kate's opinion. After the Sea and the Pyrenees I 'm sure the barge and the Brittany rivers would be very slow. Rome and the Ripa Grande for me. It has been the dream of my life to go to Italy. Do let us all go. We have had enough of the Mediæval and the Gothic for the rest of our lives. Let us have a peep at the sunny South —the vines and the orange groves—and the remains of Classic times."

"Annie, you traitress!" said Uncle Jack. "You are in league with my madcap niece. And is it really so, Kate? You prefer the sea and a longer trip,—or is the old BAGATELLE herself the great attraction? Well then, for the first year we must indulge you, I suppose. Harry—with your permission, I charter the BAGATELLE for the next year, and pay all expenses. But don't say Yes to my offer, if you mean No."

Clifford pointed, with a smile, at Kate, and said "Ask her." So Kate put her arms round her kind Uncle's neck, and whispered "It shall be Yes, of course, you dear kind Jack."

The next morning Clifford and Kate were married in the funny little old-fashioned church amongst the trees — with its new organ and painted window—and its hatchments and marble monuments inside—and its pretty churchyard, with the long wooden tomb-boards and the texts over the more humble graves without. Mr. Bell himself performed the ceremony, with much solemnity; and that dear old man, the gardener, officiated as clerk. Uncle Jack gave the bride away, and her cousin and two sisters were bridesmaids. It was quite a private wedding, and no friends were asked; but the pews and aisle were filled both with old and young from every cottage round, and many a glistening eye amongst those humble friends watched every movement of the youthful bride, and many a blessing was invoked upon her as she left the church.

And then followed the wedding breakfast; and the speeches, so simple, and affectionate, and genuinely true; and then the strangely mingled emotions of joy and sorrow, as the bride of seventeen bade farewell to the home of her infancy, her childhood, and her youth.

They were gone—but to return again in a few weeks. And then followed another and a longer parting; and Jim had work that he liked to do again; and Clifford and his lovely partner made once more a happy home on board the BAGATELLE.

THE END.